From the Windows of
Inspiration through the
Revelation of Incarceration

LETTERS TO THE LORD

FROM THE

SOUL OF JERMAINE REAVES

VOLUME ONE

JERMAINE REAVES

LETTERS TO THE LORD FROM THE SOUL OF JERMAINE REAVES
FROM THE WINDOWS OF INSPIRATION THROUGH
THE REVELATION OF INCARCERATION

iUniverse books may be ordered through booksellers or by contacting:

iUniverse
1663 Liberty Drive
Bloomington, IN 47403
www.iuniverse.com
1-800-Authors (1-800-288-4677)

ISBN: 978-1-5320-3939-3 (sc)
ISBN: 978-1-5320-3940-9 (e)

Library of Congress Control Number: 2017918919

Print information available on the last page.

iUniverse rev. date: 12/20/2017

Dear World,

I introduce myself to you with open arms and a devoted heart that my life be a teaching and a blessing to all those who read this book inspired by the Lord. My name Jermaine Lamar Reaves. I am the proud father of three beautiful children. My oldest daughter name is Jasmine Shermaine Reaves. My son name is Brandon Germail Simmons. My youngest daughter name is Brianna Jaliyah Reaves. Then there is a granddaughter by my oldest daughter her name is Jamiracle Reaves. She is a gift that I have only witness through photographs since my time of incarceration.

My mom Jeanette Reaves, and father Hubert Ingram are still living striving to maintain some normalcy through my incarceration who I miss so much. My youngest brother Christopher Reaves is a prime example of the affect this incarceration have had on my family, because like me he have struggled on, and off majority of his life dealing with incarceration. I am so grateful, because through this incarceration the Lord have kept them to still be here in my life. Even though I have not seen them throughout my seven years of incarceration. That I am finally completing on a ten year sentence. Which is apart of God purpose for my life.

I done learned a lot about my family being in a relationship with the Lord. They have also learned a lot through this incarceration about being a family. as well. Especially me as a father to my kids. So through the grace, love, and mercy from God I am in the final year of my incarceration. That I am now completing my time at Edgefield South Carolina. Which been a journey for me to go from Butner North Carolina. Then to Manchester Kentucky on to Edgefield South Carolina. So if you want to know about anything else concerning me. It will be notified and available to the world real soon.

Before I end this introduction I can't leave out the fact that I saw my youngest daughter Brianna Reaves take her first steps in the Federal Prison visiting room in Butner N.C. in 2002. That moment brung so many tears to my eyes. To just know I got seven in a half more years to go to not see her first encounters in so many more things concerning being in her life. Which is truly hurtful, and it is something I advise you all not to witness. Even though that day it was some joy mix with those tears. To just know and understand through her mom which God have bless me to have in my life through these long years of incarceration. Told me that if it's in God will she will be with me to the end. That day I didn't even realize the Lord have bless her with strength, and put faith in my heart to witness true love and respect. Due to the fact that I would have never thought in a million years a woman I treated so bad can still love me like she do. Plus be here for me like she have done. So through this journey of incarceration the Lord have bless me in so many ways and now it is my time for me through the Lord to bless my love ones and the World. This book have not been editing in ways dealing with other people, and what I mean about that. This is me, and God with a heavy anointing. That sat down on me by the Holy Spirit to write this book. So this book might have a lot of run in sentences, punctuation errors, misspelled words, and everything else, because I went off my faith in God. To not change nothing God told me to say in this book. That could have affected the anointing, and the guidance of the Holy Spirit.

SPECIAL ACKNOWLEDGEMENT

I will like to give thanks first to my Lord and Savior Jesus Christ who bless me with life and have showed me through everything I been through in life that I am truly one of his chosen vessels in the work of ministry through the calling and purpose of my life through writing these letters to the Lord from my soul. That done witness so many wrong stages of living in this world.

I also like to thank my mom and dad because if it wasn't for them I wouldn't be here to share this calling the Lord have put on my life. Mom I know you been through alot with me, and always been there for me and my brother but everything we been through was for this reason that about to happen where we can prosper in life in all the right ways. Dad even though you was in and out of my life, and wasn't there like a father should I still love you and forgive you because if it wasn't for you like I said before I wouldn't be here. So now that I am here this is the Lord work for my life.

I also want to give thanks to my soulmate Latasha Ward at this point who in my life if it in the Lord will for my life for her to be my soulmate forever. So thank you, and your family. For the love, and support, because like they say "behind every strong woman it destine to be actual fact a man of greatness". Thank you Latasha for everything, and the time you devoted your life being here for me and raising our kid. Please know that I am truly sorry, but somethings that happen in life was meant to happen for a purpose, and reason. That the Lord wanted us to go through to make us better from these trying times. Where we can reach a level of unity, and a life in due time fill with prosperity.

I like to thank God for my three beautiful kids. Your daddy have made so many mistakes in life that have affected his life, and being a father. Pleases forgive me. I am sorry, and have learned that being a parent you can't take it for granted.

Now to my brother Christopher Reaves you know we done been through enough in life dealing with all kinds of struggles, and walks of life in the streets and this incarceration. Brother it's our time to do what the Lord have put us here to do for each other and our love ones. I love you brother, and hope to see you soon.

So once again thank you Lord for everything and all things. Now you all can tune in brothers and sisters, and witness the power of the Lord. Working through my soul, and pouring out so many life changing experience being incarcerated. Plus staying in the present of the lord daily. That is leading me through a journey I never dream of are imagine for me in my life write to the world.

FOREWORD

The introductory part of this book begin with God revealing to me lead by the Holy Spirit the anointing on my life in the early years of my incarceration with the first writing of letters to the Lord.

They all began as I worked the graveyard shift from 11:30 p.m. to 6:30 a.m. when I was incarcerated at the Federal Prison Camp in Manchester K.Y. during the year 2005 at a place they call the power house. At the powerhouse all you had to keep you company was the continuous buzzing of the machinery that controls all of the lights, and energy at the prison camp. One day sitting there at work I began writing letters to the Lord, and this just came to me out of nowhere. So this book will began with my early stages of my Christian journey with the Lord. The beginning part of the book will consist of the collection of thirteen letters to the Lord. It would have been a larger collection of work, but as one of the letters will inform you early on in my journey I lost a tablet. That consist of more of my earlier stages of works in writing letters to the Lord.

Next the book will go into me maturing in writing to the Lord which is a stage where I done grew in my relationship with the Lord. Then all of a sudden for an extended period of time I totally stopped writing to the Lord, and I really can't say what really caused this. It just happen, a stumbling block came my way out of nowhere filled with so much hurt and loneliness. That made me realize a lot of things. Plus ask the lord what is going on? Something I advise you not to do, is question God. The Lord responded by just moving me back to the place in my life being committed and dedicated. That allowed me to start back writing to him about what was going on through that period of time where I had stop writing to him. Where I can readjust my focus again from that stumbling block. That allowed me to know, and understand. That what I was going through at that time dealing with so much loneliness, different stages of people I never seen, and just life on a level I didn't understand, but had to encounter. Which showed me the people you thought was going to be there for you is not there no more, and the people you thought wasn't going to be there is there. I just could not understand that at the time. So the Lord just put me back in line, because I did not understand my purpose at the time. Through the condition of the anointing the Lord of creation had blessed me with. Then at that level, and time in my life I grew to realize a lot about my calling, and purpose in life. Then my relationship with the Lord grew. My knowledge, understanding, and wisdom grew. Which started to reveal to me all the blessing from the Lord to bless other people soul, mind, and heart abundantly. That was presented to me through the Lord in many varieties of letters that I wrote to the Lord on a more matured stage.

Then the conclusion of this book going to reveal that the more I got to know the Lord the more the Lord elevated me writing these letters to him for the people of this world. So before we start in my introduction page I can't forget to mention my other family. The Reaves family, and the Ingram family. The Trawick family, and a little more details about my life. I been in and out of jail for the last sixteen years of my life. I am 31 years old at this present time. I have always struggled with a lot of choices and decisions in life. Some was dealing drugs and innumerable amount of dealing with women. That lead me to some of my life experiences and trials and tribulation. That includes me being shot two times, me being stabbed two time, and even got hit by a car at the mere age of five. Not to mention so many more trails and tribulation I can continue to name, but guess what I am still here. By the Lord grace, love, and mercy and not to forget the favorites the Lord have had on my life even when I didn't even know it. That allowed me to still be here for this reason that about to be reveal to the world like I said before.

So no more waiting people of this world, but to sum this up this is truly the reason that my journey of incarceration has been so long. Where that I can learn and grow through this relationship with the Lord after giving my life to him six years ago through my beginning stage of incarceration. That by no means been easy, because I've witness and seen so many losses in my life. Through so many changes from people who I thought love and respect me. Through it all the Lord have allowed me to grow. Plus gain the most important, and successful thing in the world I could have ever done in life, and that is being in a relationship with the Lord. That have taught me, and showed me. Molded, and shaped me. Renewed me, and kept me focused through everything dealing with my life and this incarceration. The Lord has provided me with the knowledge through these 7 years plus and gave me something I never would thought in my life could happen to a person like me. So to the world finally here is my life through these letters from my soul to the Lord from THE WINDOWS OF INSPIRATION THROUGH THE REVELATION OF INCARCERATION.

PART ONE

The beginning stages of my Christian journey
in writing letters to the Lord.

Dear Lord,

I love you, and thank you for everything. Guide, and teach me Lord to have the same attitude toward everything that happen in my life. Whether it's a good or bad situation. Which will help me by just knowing and understanding that the Lord have instilled in me great confidence and trust. To fulfill all my needs and to always stay the same. Which going to allow so many blessing in my life.

P.S. Brothers and sisters please know that every time you cry it is nothing but a cleansing moment to the soul.

Love always
your beloved child
Jermaine Reaves

Dear Lord,

I thank you for allowing me to be a lot more stronger. I still cry a lot from loneliness, because sometimes I wonder why Lord. Then I just gather my thoughts, and write about it. Which have allowed me to truly realize how much I have change. Even in the midst of my tears, and weak moments. That have let me notice my change, and the strength that I have to endure in this incarceration. Where one day I will get a chance to look back on my life to see how far I came, and wrote to you about Lord in the midst of my tears.

Love always and forever
your beloved child
Jermaine Reaves

Dear Lord,

I have been struggling on and off lately due to my lack of concentration. Which got me not really believing in myself that I am changing as a person from the inside out. It just seems like every good thing I do a bad situation comes out of it dealing with my family communication during this incarceration. Struggling with staff members with their abusive authority. Plus so many other things I can go on and on Lord complaining about from being incarcerated. From all this time I am doing from the situation I have put myself in for years.

It's just so much going on Lord dealing with these federal system policies. That sometimes they don't even go by their own policies and even make up their own one's Lord. Which is not fair, but what can you really do about it, because I don't think that some of them are even grateful to be in the job position they are in. Due to the fact from the way they treat certain inmates. Which is bias because all inmate should be treated the same. Instead of them doing their job the way it is required by helping inmates the way they should. It's like they trying to make your time harder than it is already is. Which can and have and affected me and a whole lot of brothers and sisters incarcerated around this world. Even though Lord I know I shouldn't let it stop me and make me lose focus. It just get overbearing when you trying so hard with all your heart to do the right thing, and make the best out of the time you are doing being incarcerated for years. Then on top of that theses are the things you get in return Lord that is unfair. Which is abusive authority on all levels. That is truly not right Lord.

Lord through this I know I should have more belief and faith in my heart. I know Lord that I should concentrate more as well on learning from you Lord about these situation. About prayers, people, changes, and regardless of how much you learn to do the right things through you Lord. That it is going always still be misjudging. Disrespect, lost love, lack of communication, and definitely rejection. So I ask you Lord to please guide me and help me Lord to be blessed with a full understanding. Where I want lose out on being consistent in concentrating on being a true child of the God in all the right ways. From all the hard living that appears in my life everyday. Lead me Lord to continue to worship and praise you in a true fashion with all my heart, mind, body, and soul. Please Lord make what I write to you apart of my life always.

Love always
your beloved child
Jermaine Reaves

Dear Lord,

I am so grateful for everything life has to offer. From my life of living, to my family, and everything that you created from all level of life, and all aspect of living. That at the moment my consideration for myself seem to be in a battle right now dealing with my prayers. That got me still fighting the battle of life through the struggles of being incarcerated and dealing with changes. Plus from a lot more circumstances and situations I been praying for. That seem like nothing has gotten better. So please Lord direct my steps in life and elevate me when I am praying, because I may be praying the wrong way for the wrong things. So right now Lord please help me and guide me to learn to pray for what you want for my life no matter if I like it are not. So that we all should know that you Lord truly know what is best for us all. Which will allow us to know and understand that if we don't like the outcome of our prayers. Please Lord bless our soul to learn to embrace the things you show us through our prayers no matter what it is. Thank you Lord, because I am so grateful for the prayers you have answered, and the ones to come that you will answer in due time. Until next time Lord I love you with all my heart, mind, body, and soul.

Love always
your beloved child
Jermaine Reaves

Dear Lord,

I am still on this journey of life to grow on all stages of being obedient and faithful to the best I can and the only way I know how Lord. Even though sometimes it's so hard to maintain that level of life. From so much evil you see in this world, and so much fear of being without your family. That will allow you to have more fear of dying in here being incarcerated for years, and still got more years to go.

Even though I know you Lord will help me through this journey and in the process. That will keep me growing and believing in you Lord. That will allow me to continue to put my trust and fears in your hands Lord. Which will show me that I will overcome this journey of incarceration and get a chance to see my family again. Lord please bless my son Brandon with a bless birthday and many more to come. It his birthday and he turned 13 today, and this is how I feel on it. I wrote this letter May 21, 2005 and that is day he was born on May 21, 1992.

Love always
your beloved child
Jermaine Reaves

Dear Lord,

Please forgive me for anything I have done wrong, felt wrong, and said wrong in any way. Toward the standards of life that you have taught me to obey. Through this process of becoming a true follower toward your Kingdom. Thank you Lord for blessing me to be forgiven through the Lord and Savior of this world Jesus Christ. who is the true redeemer of this world. Through his unchangeable love, grace, and mercy. That have allowed us all in this world to still be here today.

Love always and forever
your beloved child
Jermaine Reaves

Dear Lord,

It is truly a blessing and I am so grateful to be saved, to be renewed, and in preparation in this Christian journey being incarcerated for years to understand the knowledge and wisdom from the spirit of the Lord. That now dwell in me to become what you want for me to be in this world from this incarceration, and being in a relationship with you Lord. So Lord please continue to allow me the mind and heart to strive in this Christian journey forever.

Love always
your beloved child
Jermaine Reaves

Dear Lord,

Everyday I feel like I am growing the right way staying in a relationship with you Lord. That have allowed me to begin to know that you Lord have bless me to have in my soul and my life a better outlook on things concerning myself. From what I been through and what I am going through now dealing with this incarceration. That is surely getting better for me to deal with being incarcerated everyday for years. That is now allowing me to see a lot more other stages and challenges in my life that I am beginning to overcome. From me just maturing in life as a human being staying committed in my relationship with you Lord. Which now in the process Lord you have allowed me to start living on a true stage in my life. That is showing me how to get to know myself better dealing with what is my purpose and calling in life from ways I never knew, imagine, and thought of.

Love always
your beloved child
Jermaine Reaves

Dear Lord,

Right now I feel so lonely and down through being incarcerated. Then on top of that Lord I can't even communicate with my family like I want to right now and it hurt Lord. They seems so distant at time and it make me feel like they have no consideration for me Lord at the moment. At least that is how I feel from so much loneliness.

They should know that if I don't call them that I don't have any money at the time to call and it bother me. When you do not know how your love ones are doing. Which should bother them as well when they don't hear from me to know how I am doing. I think at least if they can't send me any money at the time. I feel like they should have some consideration to just write me a letter Lord.

I also know from this journey of incarceration Lord that they got to live their life as well regardless of my situation. Even though Lord I go through these stages all the time and I have learned the importance of my mistakes in life, and a whole lot of patience from being incarcerated. I have learned that life will go on with me or without me being there are not with my family. Whether I'm free are not.

So I write to you again Lord, because I feel one day someone who is going through these lonely stages of life dealing with family are whatever the case may be. who had the chance to read this letter. Will have their heart eased just like you eased mine Lord. From being in a relationship with you Lord. That will allow them to know, that you Lord will never leave us are make us feel lonely.

Then they will know if no one in their family is there for them. They will understand and know from this letter you will always be there lord with them no matter what.

Love always
your beloved child
Jermaine Reaves

Dear Lord,

Please give us the strength we need when we are down. Lift us up again Lord like you always do even when we don't even know it are deserve it. Give us also Lord the will power we need everyday to overcome saying things we going to do right, but not able to do it right. From the way it should be done right, but don't know it right. Help us Lord like you always do even when we think we are still doing something wrong, but maybe it is right Lord. Where we want get discouraged, because Lord it is so hard to strive in life and don't know. Especially coming from the stages of life we have live so long that is filled with so much unrighteousness.

Lord I hope that we all know that when Satan always trying to intervene in our life to make simple things in our life that is positive become negative. That we all should be aware that this is just the way life goes sometimes. Even though you Lord have gave us the choice and strength to make the right decision when moments like this come our way. Especially when you are trying so hard to do the right things in life from the teaching of the Lord from the definition of our unrighteousness state of living. That through certain stages of life we been through we all should still understand that sometimes positive things sometimes get negative results. I just want to say thank you Lord because you give us all we need but it is up to us do it.

Love always
your beloved child
Jermaine Reaves

Dear Lord,

I know that you are looking down on us and know everything we do. Everything we feel, everything we say, everything we know, and everything we going to change in our life.

You also know Lord how our future going to be, how our kids going to be, who our husband and wife going to be, and how we going to be in life. Lord you also know how our love going to be for people in life, and how our spiritual life is also going to be. Lord you know that I can also keep naming things forever and forever on all levels of life in any situation, circumstances, and all conditions of life. That we all should know Lord that you already know what going to happen in all of them. So please Lord guide us, teach us, and show us the true meaning of becoming the person you want us to be through all these stages of life as well as the ones I did not keep naming. Where we all will make the best out of all them. Especially the ones you want us to encounter in our journey in life.

Love always
your beloved child
Jermaine Reaves

Dear Lord,

I read today's message in the daily bread on 5/31/2006. It said don't be worrying about anything, and pray for everything. Which made me start thinking that I should have been praying all the time for everything, and not just the things I need. So since I got some understanding from the daily bread reading that day Lord. I started praying for all the things the world need on all levels of life dealing with the way we are living. Thank you Lord for that message and the messages to come as I continue to strive on this Christian journey and life being incarcerated for now over five years. I am truly grateful that I am still a work in progress. I love you Lord for allowing me to use my gifts and abilities to continue to learn to praise and worship you Lord in a true committed way. That have showed me to do it in a way that is not just for myself anymore, but for everybody in this world.

Love always
your beloved child
Jermaine Reaves

Dear Lord,

Keep me holding on to you mentally and growing spiritually to have some strength to be in a right state of mind regardless of the mistakes that I have made in my life. That have put me in this federal prison now for five in a half years. That I thought by now being in a relationship with you Lord that things could, would, and should be a whole lot better. From dealing with the people I am locked up with as well as my love ones on the outside.

Lord I still have realize in some what way regardless of how I feel sometimes are what I see are assume. That things change, people change, and doing time locked up for years, your life change, because the world do not stop for no one. So I do understand, but sometimes I don't want to understand Lord. That something do change for the best and some for the worse. No matter if you there on the outside are not. I know either way though without the Lord it won't even matter no way.

So what I'm really trying to tell the peoples in this world Lord. That whatever you trying to change unless it is the right change from what the Lord want to change in our life. That whatever it is you want to change really don't matter anyway when it is all said and done if the Lord not in it. That is why we should know and realize in due time what is important in our life that need to be change.

See for me the Lord have done so much for me and brought me through so much that now I realize the importance of change. Changes on what family means, and what life is really about. From a different outlook being in a relationship with the Lord. That I took for granted and so many other opportunities that pass me by living the wrong way. That now some of the wrong choices I made I am paying for them. Some of the wrong choices I made toward myself, my family, and so many others. That is teaching me to continue to learn everyday about change and life being in a relationship with the Lord that is so amazing, and full of the truth. That now I know I have the Lord's protection, and I can follow the Lord to make better choices. That have lead me a mighty long way dealing with so many changes that done took place in my life, my family life, and the world dealing with this incarceration. That even though I am still searching and striving to be better everyday. While in a process of learning everyday. From how to accept being away from the people I love and the changes I look forward to make. That is going to make me better from learning to want to change. Lord I am so grateful to just be alive regardless of the changes I have not made, and still struggle with being in this relationship between me and you Lord.

Love always
your beloved child
Jermaine Reaves

PART TWO

The stages of writing letters to the Lord through the
process of growth and maturity. While still striving in
this christian journey, and the path of incarceration.

Dear Lord,

I want to be at a level in my life through you Lord that when you open up the book of Jermaine Reaves the first chapter start off telling you about a man with a lost and broken soul. Who done been through so many trails and tribulation in life. That have allowed him to see so many people go through some of the same things are even worse, but through it all, the Lord have bless me to still be here.

Chapter two start with the journey of living the life of the world and those ungodly standards that the world label me as from dealing with so many different woman. That later on in my life I realize was no good for me. Having money from selling drugs. That gave me respect on the street and the little so call power you claim you have. That causes more kind of wrong living. That have you living for the wrong reason, and for the wrong things in life.

Chapter three talks about the stages of Jermaine Reaves life through being incarcerated on and off. That took so many years out my life, my kids life, and so many opportunities out my life.

Then on to chapter four which talks about coming from living in the darkness all my life to a level where I am striving with the Lord to now walk in the light. That in due time it will make a difference in my life, my family life, and the world.

Then chapter five talks about the changes of Jermaine Reaves life. From living and striving being saved, and anointed to live out the Lord will for my life. That done truly define me as a person and one of the Lord's vessel from writing to Lord for the peoples of this world.

Chapter six goes on and discuss living as a true follower of the Lord and his teaching to the best of my abilities, and the only way I know how. Through faith, with understanding, and wisdom from living on so many different wrong levels of life. Whether It was the right way, are the wrong way, because the Lord have showed me a purpose in life and my calling through writing letters to him. Which will soon be shared to many people in this world. From what I have wrote to you Lord from these experience, and all the things I have been through to get to this next chapter.

Which is chapter seven a completion stage in my life right now, and if you do not know seven mean complete. So please know this as well that I might not be complete all the way in the eyes of so many people, but I am complete in the Lord eyes in so many ways. Which is so important to me, because that is what really going to matter the most when the time come.

So no matter how you feel about the book of Jermaine Reaves life at this stage. This book is a learning process from life changes. Plus at this stage in the book of my life you should have learned a lot of things that so many people in this world go through everyday. Then on top of that there is some other important things you should have learned about the book of Jermaine Reaves. Which is to never judge a book by the cover. You should have also learned if you read this book close. That you should be getting a full understanding through each chapter in the book of Jermaine Reaves life. To please know, and learned that through being judge. God greatest children is the one they judge and characterize the wrong way.

So now when you getting to the end of the book of Jermaine Reaves life it should amaze you from some of the gifts the Lord give to people who you want believe are imagine. Also know that the Lord have put a special jewel in us all know matter who you is, what you been through, are where you come from. That if we do not use that jewel the Lord put in us the right way. It will be a cost to you, and the world. So please don't give up on yourself, because we are all a precious jewel.

Now we done got to the final chapter of the book of Jermaine Reaves life and now the world done witness the Lord power. So now I can assume a lot of people who reading this book don't want to close it, and I don't either. The Lord said, "close it for now". Where they will know after reading this book that the Lord have gave me inspiration and revelation from the Holy Spirit that my whole life have change, and this book is a blessing to the world.

P.S. Brothers and sisters

Please understand that no matter if you didn't get a chance to read this book. Had a chance to read this book, but didn't want to read this book for whatever reason. Thank you all anyway, especially the ones who did read this book, and this book help you in a lot of ways in your life. Thank you, and I give the glory to the Lord, because like I said before, "this is a true story". That was lead by the Lord. Who have taught me to know. That I am a true follower and messenger from the Lord, and this is Jermaine Reaves and the Lord book together. So it got to be true, and it had to be reveal to the world.

Love always
your beloved child
Jermaine Reaves

Dear Lord,

You already know that I am 34 years old, and so many people know me, but don't really know me Lord. The sad thing about it they have known me all my life. Then the ones who knows of me doesn't know me, but think they know me. Why Lord? I do not know, but I know this, and ask myself, how can they. When I really didn't know myself. It is bad Lord anyway from the way they think they knew me. Which is probably from what they heard are assume about me. That at the moment wasn't the real me.

Plus how many other people I didn't know who wanted to know me. Wanted to be like me, and be around me, but still didn't really know me. That affected them and my kids the wrong way. Due to the fact that they didn't know me they just love me, because I am their father. It affected my mother the same way Lord. She really doesn't know me she just know me as her son. It affected my brother the same way. It affected my daddy the same way. It affected my family the same way. It affected the women who was a part of my life the same way. It affected everyone else I didn't name the same way.

So Lord all these people think they knew me in somewhat stages in life as a father, as a brother, and as a son. As a friend, as a boyfriend, as a drug dealer, and as a bad person. As a good person, and I can keep naming the way they think they knew me. Which is sad like I said before, because they really didn't know me for real. Do it matter Lord? Yes it matter, because once they get to know the real me. Then there life will be affected the right way by the one who is really the real me. Then they can realize the true me, and the one who created me, and them too. Where everybody I name can now know me as the real me from the one who created me, and bless me to make it through all the stages I just name. Then when they get to know the real me. I will get to know the real them. Through what the Lord done did to my life to get to know myself, and know them too. Even though Lord I know I probably won't know who they are, because it is a lot of peoples who say they know me, but don't. I guarantee through you Lord in due time. They will know who I am, and the one who is truly in me.

The NIV bible says in John 17 verses 20 -23. Starting at verse 20 "My prayer is not for them alone. I pray also for those who will believe in me through their message, 21 that all of them may be one, Father, just as you are in me and I am in you. May they also be in us so that the world may believe that you have sent me. 22 I have given them the glory that you gave me, that they may be one as we are one- 23 I in them and you in me-so that they may be brought to complete unity. Then the world will know that you sent me and have love them even as you have loved me. I know you near us always Lord.

Love always
your beloved child
Jermaine Reaves

Dear Lord,

As I come to you everyday searching for a better way in life for myself, and in the process having a better understanding to stay better. From the way you have change me toward my love ones, and the people of this world. From the privilege I have receive through this process of incarceration. That was meant for me to go through. That I am so grateful to understand, and know. That so many things in my life have got a whole lot better. That have also allowed me to know that regardless of where you at in life. We will always be in the hands of God.

The hand that raise up, that even the storms obey. The hand that touch you, and you are heal in every way. The hand of the Potter hand. Which is the hand of God. The hand that mold, and shape you to reach your full potential in life. The hand that's in the the midst of the separation in family during incarceration. The hands that's in the midst of unity, and division in the churches around the world. The hand that's in the midst of the discrimination, and hatred around the world. The hand that's in the midst of all the wicked and evil we see around us everyday. The hands that if you don't know by now. The hands of the Lord is on use everyday to make it through these situations and circumstances that we maybe in right now are been in all our life.

Lord there is so many soul being lost thinking we are living on our own abilities and strength. Which allowed me to understand from this journey of incarceration when you at a stage like that putting your life in your own hands. Things will happen to you in so many of the wrongs ways you have no idea how to handle them. Then on top of that when these stages do come your way and it left in your own hands. People of this world the things you going through will never change.

So sisters and brothers, please be informed, why I am so grateful I been touch and blessed to be in the hands of the Lord. That have let me know, and now you know we don't have to put our life in the hands of ourselves, and the peoples of this world. When all we got to do is put our life in the hands of God. Please know this as well brothers and sisters once you been touched and blessed, and in the hands of the Lord. He got you where you need to be, and that is in his caring, and strong hands.

So please always hold out your hand to the next person to be touched and blessed. Where that this type of lifestyle being in the hand of the Lord will allow us all to realize and know. To live for the Lord. We must die to self as well as all the stages of life we cannot learn from any other way. By not putting our life in the hands of the Lord. Which is truly a blessing being in the hands of the Lord.

Now brothers and sisters take one moment to look at your hands. Then think about it for a second, and ask yourself "can I use my hand to stop storms". "Heal people through all things on all levels of life". "Can I use my hands to cause change", and most of all "can I use my hands like the one that created everything that exist". I think not, but some people have healing gifts in their hands for certain reason. Which could never compare to the hands of God.

Then my brothers and sisters take the time out sometimes, and just look around you at a lot of people still walking around with their hands in their pockets. I am a living witness of that, and probably we all is. So how can so many stages we go through in life be left in our hands, and expect something to change. When we walking around with them in our pockets, and got our hand in something we have no business having them in anyway. Then the sad thing about that

my brothers and sisters we can only hold so much in our hand, but
my God my Lord got the whole world in his hand.

Love always
your beloved child
Jermaine Reaves

Dear Lord,

I am at a stage in my life were that I'm maturing in your presence day by day, and night by night. That have allowed me not to be content in being positive through every trial and tribulation that I may face everyday. Even though Lord I have realize that to be incarcerated. PLus always run into struggles on top of that Lord. I have learn through them from you Lord. Now I can, and will make the right choices through these moment. Which is hard, but definitely worth it. These encounters will also make you realize the purpose in what you going through, and why you going through them. Which have only made me better, and stronger through this incarceration, and life. Which now I truly understand the things I am going through right now was not a mistake, and was meant to be. To show me that this was a recap, and a process that had to happen to me in life. Where I can open my eyes, and see the right way to live through all my trials and tribulation, and all my struggles that I needed to go through. Where I can have a better life, and continue to learn how from this long, and hard journey of incarceration.

Even though Lord I hate being locked up, and I hate I didn't keep my eyes open during all the other times I repeated being incarcerated over and over again. Lord I just pray that the world understand. That when I said "keep my eyes open". I am talking about the importance of life, and the things I should of been focus on to change during the time I was in and out of prison. That would have change my life from all the other times I repeated being incarcerated. Thank you Lord for blessing me to stay focus, and keep my eyes wide open through this ten year sentence. That I never would have thought in my life I would be locked up now going on seven years. Which have truly showed me the true, and right way to live my life. Being in a relationship with the Lord.

The NIV bible says in Deuteronomy chapter 4 verse 9 Only be careful, and watch yourselves closely so that you do not forget the things your eyes have seen or let them fade from your heart as long as you live. Teach them to your children, and to their children after them.

Love always
your beloved child
Jermaine Reaves

Dear Lord,

Life is like a puzzle. Which we all know puzzles have many
pieces, and is something you got to put together. So our life is like
a puzzle that start from birth. That is a main piece of the puzzle of
your life, but without your mom and dad together in unity raising
you from birth together a piece of that puzzle won't actually be
complete. Do not get me wrong, because a lot of parents raise their
kids without a father being there or a mom being there. Which is
why a lot of the conditions of the puzzles in our life, and the world
are in the wrong place. Which can, and have cause so many of us
in the world many problems, and so many wrong decisions in life.

Though the Lord push a lot of us to move on, and put a woman
in that place for a mom, are a dad. Then again it can be the opposite
way. Are it may be a man in the same place he put that woman in if
you know what I mean. What if drugs was put in that place, being
in a gang was put in that place, and basically all negative pieces of
life that goes on everyday in life put in that place. That we all sit
back as people of this world let goes on dealing with the pieces of the
puzzle in our life. That just been put in so many of the wrong place.

Then now you do not have that piece of the puzzle in your
mind in the right place, because it done been put in the wrong place,
because of neglect and abuse. Then the heart pieces of the puzzle is
now missing, because it is in the wrong place hardened by love, and
so much negativity from the mistakes, and failures we continually
make. Then the soul pieces of the puzzle in the wrong place that is
fill up with a lot of confusion, and uncertainties. Now your life puzzle

is all over the place in so many of the wrong things. The heart in the wrong place where the mind should be. The mind in the wrong place where the soul should be. The soul in the wrong place where the heart should be, and now the whole puzzle of your life is totally messed up.

Which now you got to start the whole puzzle over again, and now your life have been through so many trials and tribulations that done lead many of our brothers and sisters to death. That includes love ones, and all.

So let's go back, and look at the puzzle of your life. To still know, and understand this. That no matter if all the pieces was in the right place, and your life still end up all over the place, and still messed up. Why? because we did not have the main piece of the puzzle which is the Lord and Savior of this word Jesus Christ. That will allow all we go through, for us to know that all it take is to be in a relationship with him, and to be born again. From a different birth through our Lord and Savior Jesus Christ who died, and resurrected for the sin of this world. Where we can, and will understand. That through this we can live through the things he show us, teach us, and want us to live through. If we follow his instruction, and guidance. Being committed and dedicated to understand what it truly mean to be born again. So that the puzzle of your life want only be put together the right and proper way. It will definitely be complete, and every piece of the puzzle of your life will be in the right, and proper place.

Then on top of that everything around you will also be put together as well in the right, and proper place by the Lord through the way your life was meant to be through his will. Plus after that then you can look back on your life when the puzzle is complete, and put together by the Lord, and you should say "thank you Lord for making me a great masterpiece of a true child of God".

Love always
your beloved child
Jermaine Reaves

Dear Lord,

My brother in Christ came to me and ask me why "things always happening the wrong way in his life after all he do is strive to do the right things". After everything he already going through dealing with these hard, and trying time from this incarceration? So I explain to him in so many ways about why, but I wanted to make sure Lord. So like I always do Lord I ask you to lead, and educate me to write this letter for him, and all the rest of my brothers, and sisters of the world going through these same stages are worse. Where we all can know why wrong things always happening to us. While we are striving to always want to do the right things, and while we already going through some hard, and trying time.

So the Lord inform me to write this letter. To let him know, and the rest of the world know that what we feel in our heart is true, and for a reason. Where we can understand that we claim all we do is right, but still everything seems to go wrong. Plus a lot more of the wrong things still going on in our life on top of the other things that are already going wrong. Which in the process we are steady doing right Lord, and this is what still happening to us for no reason. Then the Lord told me to let your brother know as well as the world. To be reminded of our ancestor Jobs story in the bible. Then the Lord also said, "he wanted us to understand, and share this to each other, and to let go of why". Where that we can put our faith in the Lord, and let the Lord handle why, and everything else that you wonder why. Where we can start accepting the things you can do to change the wrong that going on in our life instead of complaining, and worrying about it. Through us questioning things that going to happen to us regardless of the fact that we think we doing the right thing or the wrong thing.

So please understand doing the wrong thing will make it a lot harder than doing the right thing. So why do it? After you all already complaining about you doing the right thing, and still the wrong things happening. Then the Lord told me to go tell your brother, and the world this, and ask them this question. "What if everything you do right, and everything that happen to you will be right?" You think you complaining now. This world, and the peoples of the world will be worser than it already is, and that includes everything, and everybody.

So please leave the way life goes to the Lord, and follow his direction. By staying obedient, discipline, dedicated, and determine. The exact way from how life going to go, because it is nothing we can do about it, but listen to the Lord. That going to help us always through these stages. Especially if you going through these stages still doing the right thing. That going to always come your way for no reason. So now that we all know this. The Lord said to tell you all, "don't ever question him why." Just ask question, and keep doing the right thing no matter if we think the wrong things are happening.

Love always
your beloved child
Jermaine Reaves

Dear Lord,

You gave me a thought that I wonder have anyone else ever thought about in this world, and that thought was. What if you was the only person living in this world? What will we learn from Lord? Who would we talk to Lord? What will we work for to be in life Lord? How will our emotion be like considering love Lord, and on top of that what will we show love toward Lord? If we was the only one living in the world. Also what can you think about Lord? Plus what can you look forward in doing in life as well Lord?

Then I realize when I thought about this, and asking these questions Lord. I just wanted the world to know. Don't think you can do things by yourself, or want to be by yourself. So we all can just take the time out of our life to look at the condition of this world now, and be grateful.

Even though we are living in the last day's Lord. The world still and will get a chance to get a full understanding of this letter. Where they can know, and understand that. This is how it feels sometimes being locked up for so many years. That you the only one living in this world. It is a empty feeling sometimes, because you don't know what to expect, and look forward to when you do get out.

I know this though I wouldn't want to be living in this big world all by myself. So Lord that is why I pray to you like we all should do everyday. Where I can know I am not by myself, because no matter if we are around people everyday living in this world we still can be along. That is why I am so grateful Lord that I take the time to look around me everyday, and appreciate you Lord for your perfect creation, and everything that came with this creation whether I like it are not.

P.S. You think we get lonely at time. Just imagine my brothers and sisters living in this world all by yourself.

I truly submit and surrender
my soul to you always
Jermaine Reaves

Dear Lord,

I am sitting here in my cube in a moment where I feel so inspired about my life regardless of me being incarcerated. That sometimes it make me feel like I am so different that I cannot even identify myself at certain parts of the day. Especially on some days when I am devoting my time with you Lord to grow stronger from the divine presence I feel from the Holy Spirit that send chills all over my body Lord. That is so inspirational on a level that I don't even realize what's going on around me.

Which on them days Lord I just have a feeling on me in that moment that is not explainable, but expressible without explanation. That have me fill with so much inspiration from the spirit of the Lord that have manifested my soul to be exalted in a movement that going to cause a complete change in the world in due time through the power of the Lord. That going to inspire this whole world through the Lord using me to revive the life of the peoples of this world from the inspiration of the gospel. That this world want even understand, and comprehend.

So through this movement that going to take place in due time in the world from the Lord using me. Peoples of this world can get ready to just be identified as our true self. That will be inspired from a willing vessel you never would have ever thought would be truly living as a child of the Lord. That is so inspired by the gospel of the Lord. That going to be unified, and complete from the inspiration from the spirit of the Lord. From a complete, and miraculous change from the things that he use to do. To what he now do, and was born to do for the world. That going to inspire us all, and touch people life in so many ways that this world have never seen in a person like they way he use to be.

2 Timothy chapter 3 verses 16-17 says : 16 All scriptures is given by inspiration of God, and is profitable for doctrine, for reproof, for correction, for instruction in righteousness: 17 That the man of God may be perfect thoroughly furnished unto all good works.

Complete me and inspire me
always Lord your beloved child
Jermaine Reaves

Dear Lord,

It is truly a blessing, and a honor to praise, and believe in your words Lord. That have bless me to proceed in life with a reform, reshape, renewed, and repaired heart, mind, body, and soul. That have allowed me to glorify, magnify, and give you the praise, and honor. In every way, and in everything you want me to do, and accomplish striving to do the right thing in life. Everyday, all the time, always, and forever.

Love always
your beloved child
Jermaine Reaves

Dear Lord,

I do not know why, and I do not know where to begin to ask you why? Then I realize it is not up to me to ask no questions concerning the things you want me to do with my life through you Lord. I know you know through me being denied to go home again through the appeal process I filled back to the courts. That was denied, and then I was denied the drug program, because of a charge I was convicted of in 1991 Lord. Here it is now 2008, and that will make that charge almost 16 years old Lord. Then Lord the sad thing about that they want even take it off my record. Which caused my appeal to be denied. That stop me from getting a early release after over 7 years of incarceration. It just didn't hurt me Lord it hurt my family, because I would have been able to go home a little earlier.

Lord you know at that point I just wanted to give up, but I didn't like a lot of my brothers I was incarcerated with thought I did. I did start having a few encounters that could have got me in trouble. Then on top of that I started lacking on going to church, and doing some of the other positive things I was doing for people dealing with working out, and ministering. So evidently all my brothers was right. Plus they all was there for me to encourage me. Which I was so grateful to be around great men of God. That kept encouraging me. That really help me get stronger, and closers to you Lord. Which also allowed me to strive harder to keep on doing what I know is right regardless of these trying time.

In the process of all this I receive the drug program. The thing about that though, I can go, but I cannot get anytime off. Due to fact of me being denied from that 16 year old charge. Regardless of the fact it did put me in a position to help myself, but take up a space from someone one else who can get in the program to go home earlier. It hurt me, but I allowed myself to move out the way to let one of the other brother go ahead, and get in the program. Even though he was just locked up a little over a year.

The point is Lord you love when we make these type of sacrifices sometimes for people. Even though I was not going to get no time off, but it would of showed the people who determine me getting out. That I was really striving to better myself. Which would have allowed more halfway house time, and faster paperwork filled out for me to get out a lot quicker, because my paperwork would have been in process sooner than it should have.

So through this journey whether you incarcerated are not we got to make some sacrifices for God, and toward peoples. Plus the Lord want me to inform you all again never question him about nothing. He knows what best, and the Lord will put people around you no matter where you at, and what you are going through. So from that point on I just felt different when I prayed, and studied. That allow me to realize I wasn't at a level with the Lord like I thought I was.

It bothered me, because the faith that the Lord gave me I thought I was finished being incarcerated and my calling was about to be released to the world. I was about to unite back with my family where they can witness what the Lord have lead me through, but it did not happen at that moment. I learned, and realize that something we go through we will never know, and understand why. That things like this continue to happen to us.

I do know this at that point a lot happen to my soul, and heart. A slight tear cut into my heart, and soul that allowed a lot of different wrong feelings, and ways build up inside of me. That I wanted to question the Lord about, and ask why? After all what I was going through at the moment. In the midst of it all that tear in my heart, and soul did not heal all the way, and all I can say at that point is why me Lord? After all these years the things you lead me through I am still incarcerated. After all the prayers, and opportunities through these new laws to give brothers, and sisters like myself another opportunity to return back to our family a little earlier.

Then that is when the spirit of the Lord took over them weak thoughts in my mind, soul, and heart and made me realize it is not about me no more. That sacrifice you made for that brother. The peoples you done help lose weight, and ministered to. That is what it about being a true servant no matter what you have to go through. On top of that it is not about what you think, and how you feel. Where you at, and how life have been in the past, and now. It is about the future through the ones the Lord bless that going to be apart of me, and my life.

Then I thought about it, and ask the Lord another question? "How can they reach their full potential in life with no guidance Lord"? Then the Lord let me know again, and it was clearly with authority that some things you will never understand. Then I realize through the changes I was bless with to overcome that my kids, my family, and the outside world didn't see, because of this incarceration for now 7 years. That the power of the Lord through the holy spirit let me know that I he can do anything that we don't understand, are see, and ever know. Plus the Lord made me realize too that some things I make happen in our life was meant to happen through what you going through in life to reach your kids, and the people who is affected by your life through me the Lord and Savior of this world. Whether you're there with them are not.

So Jermaine if you know me like you say you know me you will know why you still incarcerated. I am the Lord who know what best for you. I know everything, because everything is me. The Lord also told me I know your love ones need you, but the Lord need you to Jermaine. Where you will understand through me the Lord that you are one of my sanctified vessel, and the anointing that lay inside of your heart, and soul which wasn't torn like you thought it was. You will now know why you still incarcerated, because I was not finished with you yet. When I finish, and send you home the whole world will know why it took so long.

P.S. Before you close this letter the Lord said to inform the world this. "Do not never question him, and ask him why", because he know why, and they will too.

John chapter 8 verse 14 say; 14 Jesus answered and said to them, Even if I bear witness of myself, my witness is true: for I know where I came from, and where I am going: but you do not know where I came from and where I am going.

Psalm chapter 27 verse 13 and 14 reads; 13 I would have lost heart, unless I had believed; That I would see the goodness of the Lord. In the land of the living. 14 Wait on the Lord. Be of good courage, and he shall strengthen your heart; wait, I say on the Lord.

Psalm chapter 37 verses 23 and 24 reads; 23 The steps of a good man are ordered by the Lord; and he delights in his way. 24 Though he fall, he shall be utterly cast down; For the Lord upholds him with his hand.

Love always and forever
your beloved child
Jermaine Reaves

Dear Lord,

I know through my life I been so blessed to make it through so
many storms in my life by your love, and mercy Lord. Even when I
didn't know it. I am talking about the storms in life Lord. Where the
rain came, and flooded my soul with so much violence, negative,
hurts, and trials and tribulation Lord. That it got to a point where
I was drowning in so much unrighteousness. That was leading me
to a place where I was either going to die or be incarcerated for the
rest of my life. In that flood I also was seeing a lot of my brothers,
and sisters drowning as well.

Then in the storm through the flood the thunder, and lightning
struck my heart with so much brokenness, and losses. That had
me wanted to give up on life especially when that brokenness, and
everything else I was going through lead me to a road I knew in
due time probably was going to happen. Which was the taking of
my liberation through being incarcerated for so many years on a 10
year sentence.

Before that the storm came, another storm was already at a
pace through the forces of a tornado. That done come through,
and destroyed our neighborhoods with drug, gangs, and all type
of other disasters. That went on in the tornado winds that got
stronger, and caused so much death, so much much animosity, so
much hatred, and jealousy.

Now the tornado done turned into a hurricane. Which not only
coming through stronger and stronger destroying everything from
the condition of the hurricane. That Is now hitting our homes,

and family relationships. The community, and the church. That is causing so many problems with each other. The division in the church is getting worser. The discrimination in the world is worser. Then all this hatred, and envy among each other have gotten worser. The separation, and problems with our kids, our sister, and brother. The relationship dealing with marriage, friends, and all family. PLus not to mention the most important thing we can ever have in life, and that is a relationship with the Lord.

See these type of storms in life keep us from being in a relationship with the Lord anyway. So as we try to work through the these type of storms. We all got to have that relationship with the Lord. Do your life when these storms come will take you away from here.

That is why we got to understand that we all need the Lord. Which remind me about the story in the bible in the book of Genesis about Noah, and the ark. God told him to build the ark the way God wanted it. Which took obedience, and faith. To help save his family, and everything that was around him, because a storm was coming that will wash you away if you don't listen, and obey the Lord.

That is why it is so important to be in a relationship with the Lord. Staying obedient, and faithful. It will allow you you to know that the Lord can put things, and people around you when these storms come. That will keep you safe from any storm you face in life. The Lord is that one you can call on, and he is always there through every storm we face in life. Whether we know it are not. To protect us from so many different kind of storms that try to keep us from reaching our full potential in life.

So threw his spirit we live on through him. Who protect us, and guide us to move on through all type of storms of life, and everything else that try to get in our way. Especially if we striving with the Lord living through his guidance, and preparation. That will lead us through anything we face, and go through. The Lord is everything not just something. Especially the things that happen in our life that we see are don't see. So now if you don't know, now you know that God put us in a position to always overcome any storm we face in life. It is just up to us to accept that position. Have no fear, and believe in the Lord.

P.S. My brothers and sisters. We all should know that we all have been through so many storms in life. Still going through some, and will always go through some. Just know that every time they come our way make the right choice through them, and let the Lord lead you. To give you the opportunity to make it through them. So they want have a chance to take your life away before your time, and if you will please get your bible.

Please read in Mark chapter 4 verses 35 through 41. Where you can be a witness. That even by the raising of his caring hand no storms in life will not stand up to the Lord.

Love always
your beloved child
Jermaine Reaves

Dear Lord,

    As I sit in my cube, and write in the dark in the wee hours of the morning. Due to my respect of cutting on the light, and disturbing the brothers incarcerated around me. I know in the morning when I read what I wrote being led by the Holy Spirit. That light going to shine forth no matter if I didn't see our know what I was writing. I know writing this in the dark, and expressing myself to you Lord. When the morning come I can see what I wrote, and someone eyes will be open with understanding.

    So whoever reading this. This is what I wrote what you reading. Using my spiritual eyes which dwell in us all. After whoever is reading this letter you will feel the blessing that is a gift in us all if we use it the right way. From writing in the dark lead by the Holy Spirit that made sense from using one of my gift from God by writing this letter in the dark, but made sense when you read it in the light. That is so unique in a way that no matter what I write in the dark are write in the light. The glory of the Lord will shine forth, and open the eyes of others when you are reading this letter to experience the Lord amazing gifts in us all. That will allow us all to know that we all can read in the light, but we can't definitely read nothing in the dark, but we sure will understand everything that is a message from the Lord whether you can see it are not. So no matter what you write in the dark with your eyes open, are in the light with your eyes closed. It will always have understanding, and a purpose. When you are using your gifts from God the right way lead by the

Holy Spirit. Which is our spiritual eyesight and understanding. From things we assume we can't see are understand.

Love always
your beloved child
Jermaine Reaves

Dear Lord,

You, and I both know through your teaching, and understanding that you have bless me to have in my mind. To know, and take heed that the devil work all day everyday. Which had me thinking if he ever take a break someone's life will be better. Then again to the knowledge I have been bless with in this growing process in my life on this Christian journey in a true relationship with the Lord. No matter how hard he work. When the time comes. We as people in this world will realize all that hard work the devil have done is for nothing. Especially when you living in a committed relationship with the Lord. That is preparing you daily until that day come when the Lord bring us home forever. So we can relax, and understand that the devil have truly work himself to death already for nothing.

Revelation chapter 20 verses 1 through 3 says 1 Then I saw an angel coming down from heaven, having the key to the bottomless pit, and a great chain in his hand. 2 He laid hold of the Dragon, that the serpent of old, who is the devil, and Satan, and bound him for 1000 years, 3 and he cast him into the bottomless pit, and shut him up, and set a seal on him, so that he should deceive the nation know more, till the thousand years were finished: but after these things he must be released for a little while.

P.S. My brothers, and sisters. I just want you all to know this again. That if we stay in our relationship with the Lord the right, and true way. What can Satan do again, beside like he did before work himself to death again. Hopefully this time though. He will have sense enough to stay in heaven, and don't get cast out to run the world to and fro. For years, and for nothing.

Love always
your beloved child
Jermaine Reaves

Dear Lord,

Remember me when the time come so I will not be left behind no more, and I hope, and pray Lord none us do, but I know Lord a lot of us will. So as peoples of this world let us stop being so weak at time. Which is natural, and well needed some time, but not all the time. Depending on when that moments come that we can't do nothing about. That will allow you to feel lost, and wanting to give up. Paul said, in the bible that "God has sovereignty planted evidence of his existence in the very nature of us all." Then I say, "what is that when you so lost, and really don't know, and understand it Lord."

So as I matured in this relationship with you Lord. I done learned that we got everything. Even the things we don't know or understand. Which we got to realize that. Plus also know that without the Lord we got nothing, but a lost soul that done already gave up.

So Lord remember me through all the complaining, and through all my failures. All my mistakes, and everything I ever done wrong Lord. Where that through these stages in my life I had no idea, and would have never thought or knew that I was going to make it. So now that I know Lord I made it, because of you leading me, and guiding me to still be here to say," Lord remember me" So I will know, and understand Lord that when that time come I wouldn't even have to ask that question no more. Remember me, because I can remember, and the Lord my witness once upon a time ago in my life that question didn't even matter.

Luke chapter 23 verses 42 and 43 say 42 Then he said to Jesus,

Lord, remember me when you come into your kingdom. 43 And Jesus said to him, assuredly I say to you, to day you will be with me in paradise.

Love always
Your beloved child
Jermaine Reaves

Dear Lord,

Thank you for leading me to continue to strive on the path of righteousness. Evidently like you done taught me Lord to know when you choose this path, and follow my directions it is not going to be easy. So when we open our mind up to understanding, and think about the way the world is. So many people want to be on this same path, because it is available to everybody. On this path I know that when we get on this path to want to change our life from the wrong path we was living in, it seem like things in our life get a lot worser. There come more temptation, more trials and tribulations, and all types of other living condition just start to come our way that we never thought. From the way we done lived from the wrong way that happen to us that we sometimes cannot help.

Instead of us continuing on the path of righteousness with the help of the Lord through these situations. Make us start trying to go around these living conditions, and that is when the wrong way of life happens a lot worser than it already is. So then we start going to left. Then when that way of life is not working, and cannot help you. We turn, and go right. Then when the right way not helping you also. Now you turn to the Lord. Then the Lord tell us, all we got to do is follow his direction, and go straight. Where he will lead you, and keep you on the path of righteousness.

So all my life like I know a lot of us took the wrong path Lord. That most of the time lead us to a lot of hurts, separation, sickness, incarceration, and a lot more other ungodly stages of life. That even lead a lot of our brothers, and sisters to death.

So fortunately Lord I was blessed, and save through all those wrong path I took in life. That have gave me a opportunity to learn not to go left or right, but to strive by the guidance of the Lord. Which will lead me on the straight, and narrow road to eternity. So Lord like you have told me, and I am going to tell the world this path is not easy, but it is the right choice, and the Lord said" that he will be with us all the way."

Which is a honor, and a curse from the divine power of the Holy Spirit from our Lord and Savior Jesus Christ to share this letter to my brothers, and sisters. So they will all know that the path of righteousness is only so wide, but it is always room to move over to the side for the next brothers, and sisters of this world. Who is willing to want to walk it with you side by side. So please brothers, and sisters understand this, we are all God's children no matter what path we took in life. So please come on with me brothers, and sisters, and try this path of righteousness which is the right, and straight way of life. Which will lead us to eternity. Even though we all going to need help walking this journey just in case we decide to want to go to the right or go to the left. The Lord is always available, but are we going to be available to follow the Lord direction.

I love you Lord, and please keep me available with the mind to obey your direction that you want for me in my life. Thank you Lord for always showing us the right way to go where we won't get lost. Even though I know that a lot us will get lost, and will never walk the right way in life. Even when the lord done showed us which way to go. It is sad, but it is true that our choices is going to send so many of our brothers, and sisters straight to hell the right way from the wrong way many of them have lived.

Your beloved child
Jermaine Reaves

Dear Lord,

As I sit back, and realize something in my life when I was out there in the world selling drugs, sleeping with all those different women, being shot two times, and so many other dangerous, and life threaten moments. I just want people to realize that I can't even understand are imagine sometimes the way that I was living. Which now I can say that I am so grateful Lord to still be here today. From the amazing love, and mercy from you Lord. To share my testimony through writing these letter to the world through you Lord. About my life from everything I been through, and still going through.

Then on top of that Lord I can recall a lot of time a lot of people told me that I was not going to be nothing are nobody. I am going to go to jail, and guess what brothers and sisters some part of that statement was true I went to jail, and been in jail for almost 7 years now. Then again some of that statement was definitely wrong also.

See the Lord have taught me to know I will always be something, and somebody. The Lord also told me to tell you brothers, and sisters we are all somebody to someone especially the Lord. We are also here for a reason no matter what people say are think, and even after all we been through. So who cares what the people of this world thinks, because what matters the most is what the Lord know, and want for our life, and who we is. That include them same peoples also, and like I said before. "We are all somebody", even those same peoples who said, "we are nobody, and going to never be nothing."

So please know brothers, and sisters we are all the Lord beloved children. Which mean we are somebody. Now back to the statement. Truthfully, I did go to jail, but it wasn't because of what they said, it was about what the Lord wanted me to go through. Where those same peoples who said I wasn't going to be nothing to understand through the Lord that we all are something, and somebody.

Plus the way that life goes. May be one day Lord those same people will read this letter our listen to this letter being read, and realize that same person they said wasn't going to be nothing truly was somebody. That may have help them change some things in their life from that statement. If they did not get a chance to read this book or listen at this book being read. Trust me, the result was not what they said, it was what the Lord plan to happen to me any way. Which was to go to jail, and establish my life in a relationship with the Lord for those same people to understand who the Lord truly called me to be. I know you near us always Lord.

Love always and forever
your beloved child
Jermaine Reaves

Dear Lord,

Everyday striving to be a true child of God on this Christian journey along with just the journey of life in general. It is always something that going to test you along the way. Especially if you striving living the right way. So trust me, because there always will come a time for a test in life. Whether it's a test of character. A test of faith. A test of love. A test of attitude, and emotions. A test of obedience. A test of temptation, and I can keep name all other kind of tests we go through everyday on all levels of life. That have allowed the people of this world to go through everyday, and still make the wrong decision. While striving, and walking in faith with the Lord. Who have showed us all the answer to every test we face. Which all we got to do is follow the Lord teaching. From the word the Lord spoke in the bible. Which will give you every answer to the test you face in life everyday. So we cannot make an excuse when we fail, because all the answers to the test of life we face everyday. The answer are right there in the book of life, and the other answers come from all the wrong answer we make to the test of life we continue to repeat. Plus on top of that we got the best teacher in the world our Lord and Savior Jesus Christ.

Truly submit and surrender my soul to you Lord
always and forever
Jermaine Reaves

Dear Lord,

It is truly a blessing to know you, and to know that you have bless me through the spirit from the Lord with a gift to be so creative in a special way. That not only going to affect this world through you using me as one of your anointed vessel Lord but will also affect my kids to be bless as well through you Lord. Where they can have that effect on the world as well.

Lord I am so grateful, because Lord you have adjusted my soul to know writing these letters to you for the world is my purpose, and your will for my life, and a good opportunity through these stages that my kids can build a relationship with you also Lord. For my kids to establish their own purpose you want for their life as well through me from you Lord, because it is in my mind, heart, and soul to vow to you Lord. That I continue to live by your principles as a father, and a child of God with all the righteousness that have been instill in me through this journey of life from this incarceration. That won't only affect my kids Lord, but my kids can affect other kids around the world through you using me, and working through me to work through them. Where that your spirit Lord can work through us all.

Lord it is also important for us all to know Lord, and especially our kids to know that they are here in this world for a reason lord just like we all are. Regardless of what we have done, and what we been through.

So I leave my life, and my kids life into your hands Lord. That they will be blessed to understand that reason why they're here still striving in life without their father through you Lord. Where they will continue to go through the thing they got to go through in life to get them where they need to be in life dealing with me being incarcerated for so many years being out their life. Plus all the other things they been through without their father that I don't know about, but I know you know Lord. Where that the calling, and purpose that about to take place in due time through me, and my kids from the Holy Spirit that going to change the condition of the way this generation is living in.

Psalms chapter 27 verse 13 says "13 I would have lost heart, unless I had believed. That I would see the goodness of the Lord in the land of the living".

Proverb chapter 22 verse 6 also says "6 Train up a child in the way he should go: and when he is old, he will not be depart from it".

Proverbs chapter 20 verse 7 says "7 The righteous man walks in his integrity, his children are blessed after him."

Thank you Lord for always being near us, and our kids even when we don't know it, and they don't either.

Love always
your beloved child
Jermaine Reaves

Dear Lord,

It been a long hard journey in life for me, but through it all Lord I know it is about that time for a divine moment of completion in my life Lord. From this incarceration, and me being save now for six years, and incarcerated for seven years almost.

That now I am at a stage in my life where some these peoples have the nerve to say I am fool, and still continue to throw stones at me. Then Lord on top of that I been rejected a lot of ways from peoples, because of a lot of ways I have changed my life Lord. Which is causing more stones to be thrown my way. Plus Lord a lot of peoples still assume I am the same person I used to be. Which is so disrespected, because I have changed from the person I used to be, and still everyday I got to keep dodging those stones that keep being thrown at me.

Not to mention I am still being neglected, because I have changed from the person I used to be, and it seem like the stones are being thrown more. That is so painful, and the most hurting part of that pain is that a lot of people act like they don't even recognize my change, but still recognize the person I used to be.

So Lord I realize through these changes, and this growing process of me maturing in life striving in this Christian journey, and incarceration. That you Lord have taught me to know don't worry about what people think, and to realize that you Lord know my true changes that you Lord have help me make, and that is what matter the most.

Thank you Lord for helping me to want to change more, and to let me know to never stop wanted to change more no matter how many people are throwing stones at me. Thank you also Lord that you have allowed me to learn also that evidently I am doing something right if they keep throwing stones at me, because I have change for the best. So brothers, and sisters please know this, and truly understand that all them stones they done threw at me all my life didn't do nothing, but really help me heal better, and better. That also made me stronger, and stronger from so many kinds of wounds we all go through in life from them stones that come from all angles in life. That really didn't do nothing else, but make me closers to you Lord. which was the best thing I ever could have done in life.

So the closers I got to you Lord the more I start realizing, and receiving a lot of prosperity from a lot of different things I was changing in my life. I started to understand my calling, and then I realize the will the Lord want for me in my life dealing with me changing from so many things I been through, and going through now from being save, and sanctified through this journey of incarceration.

So now that I am at this level in life Lord to start understanding a lot more about change. Those same stones them people threw at me all my life Lord. You have taught me to pick some of them up, and to know that I can't, and you Lord will not let me pick up all of them, but you will Lord will let me pick up some of them. Then lead me to take them back to some of them same peoples, and say" thank you for throwing them stones at me". For this reason you are reading now. Which have showed me the truth about myself, and bless me to be in a relationship with you Lord. That have gave me everything I never thought I will ever have through this incarceration dealing with me being saved, and writing letters to you Lord in the process.

I love you, and thank you always Lord for allowing me to endure those stones they threw at me.

Love always
Your beloved Child
Jermaine Reaves

Dear Lord,

What is the greatest thing I can be blessed with to help change the world through you Lord using me as a glorified vessel. Beside me being anointed, and being sanctified by the power of the Holy Spirit, the father, and the son Jesus Christ the Lord and Savior of this world. Which is call Trinity, and that live throughout this world.

That have affected my life to even have the knowledge, understanding, and wisdom to want to be save, and blessed to help change the world through Trinity. Which is working through me to be better in life on every level everyday.

Especially from the life that I done lived that was wrong for a long time.

So through this process of being saved all I want to do is allow Trinity to use me to help the world through Trinity from what Trinity did for the world for us all to be here today. Through his son our Lord and Savior Jesus Christ. Where we can know that through his son Jesus Christ we can help the world by understanding what he did for the world from the day he was born through Trinity.

So to answer that question Lord. What can I be bless with to help change the world through you using me as a glorified vessel? That answer should be so simple to us all. Which is Trinity.

Love always
your beloved child
Jermaine Reaves

Dear Lord,

Sometime I cannot even believe my thoughts. Especially Lord when I'm sitting in my cell devoting my time with you Lord studying the word of God. Then all of a sudden the thought of me selling drugs again appeared in my mind for no reason Lord. Plus not to mention them feelings came across my thoughts like always about women. That tried to arouse my desire, and imagination with all type of wrong thoughts. That lead to so many other thoughts that just started to try to cloud my mind for no reason Lord.

Then I got to appoint where I couldn't even finish my devotional time with you Lord. I started to feel so guilty, and it hurt me, because I can't understand why these thoughts in my life at that moment appeared. Especially when I am studying the word of God.

It made me feel so ashamed, and also made me feel so disrespectful Lord, because I supposed to have my mind, and my thoughts on that devotional moment with you Lord. That is so important to my life being in your presence Lord, and being inspired in my life during this time that is well needed in the life of us all. Which will soon or later if we keep devoting our time to you Lord. We will be able to overcome these ways, and thoughts Lord. That is trying to make us kind of confuse, and just so hard to comprehend, and accept.

So please Lord allow me a full understanding to share with the world when times like this come our way. Where we can have the solution to overcome these thoughts, and stay focus on our devotional time, and study. That is so important to our life, and that will lead us to not take our mind off you Lord, and off your words. Where these thoughts want try to make me feel I cannot help myself after all the Lord have brought me through, and taught me. Even though what the Lord brung me through, and taught me. I still wonder sometimes where in the world these thoughts come from. Especially at that time when I am focusing, and trying to devote my life to you Lord by learning, and studying your words. Elaborating on some time of peace, trying to find understanding, and searching for wisdom, and change Lord.

So like I said before after all the prayers, all the preparation, all the the guidance, and all the love, and mercy you done showed me in my life Lord, and this world. It still scare me Lord, because I just do not understand my thoughts, and how it can still be like this.

Even though through it all, I do know this Lord. That you do not want me to fear nothing, but you Lord. Which will allow fear to come being in a committed relationship with you Lord.

So please Lord I ask that you put more confident in me, and also put more strength in me to overcome these thoughts, and anything else that's trying to take my mind to the wrong place. Where that I will stay encouraged with honesty, and faith. That will allow me to grow, and mature with all the true characteristics of being a God fearing man, with a right soul with all the right thoughts.

I also know that I am not going to be perfect, and some more thoughts of wrong things going to appear for no reason again and other times of the day for the rest of my life, but these experiences is preparing me for them. Where I can be ready for them through the Lord, because I do not want to always carry this fear around. That having you feeling guilty from something you can't help.

So after this long hard journey of incarceration, and Christian journey that I strive in every day to even be considering myself a God fearing man. I got to be ready to overcome these thoughts, and any other moment that come my way with the right mind frame, and the right spirit from the Lord.

Where the world will know that these are just my thoughts, and we been taught to know that the Lord move in mysterious ways. From all types of situations, and peoples to full fill the things that need to be done through you Lord. That will always be a blessing to world. That will always allow us to be better.

So like I said before, "these are still my thoughts", but I'm sure one day I will understand. So I will be prepared for them, and have better control over them, and everything else the Lord allow me to deal with. Where I will be at a level in life to never ever want to stop striving, and searching for full understanding, knowledge, and wisdom in life through you Lord that going to give me everything I need in life regardless of what my thoughts is. Especially if I can overcome them doing the will of the Lord for my life.

Proverbs Chapter 16 verses 2 and 3 says, "2 All the ways of a man are clean in his own eyes; but the Lord weigheth the spirits. 3 Commit thy works unto the Lord, and thy thoughts shall be established.

Isaiah Chapter 55 verses 7 through 9 says, "7 Let the wicked forsake his way, and the unrighteous man his thoughts: and let him return unto the Lord, and to our God, for he will be abundantly pardon. 8 For my thoughts are not your thoughts, neither are your ways my ways, saith the Lord. 9 For as the heavens are higher than the earth, so are my ways higher than your ways, and my thoughts than your thoughts.

PART THREE

The stages of my life through this incarceration being bless to truly understand my calling, and purpose in life on a whole other level. From the teaching of the holy spirit, and the anointing that God have place on my life to know that their is true greatness in me from God. That the people in this world would have never imagine.

Dear Lord,

I just wrote to the world today a short letter that the Lord put on my soul about weakness, and struggles. So please read carefully my brothers, and sisters. Where we all can get a full understanding from these stages from the Lord using me to write this letter.

When we are struggling we sometime become weak from that struggle. Which most of the time causes us to lose focus, and make some wrong choices in life Lord. So Lord I want my brothers and sisters to know, and understand father God that we should not block our blessing with the struggles we go through in life from being weak.

So brothers, and sisters please take this advice the Lord taught me to share to you all. That the wisdom to know, and understand, that every struggle we go through is for a purpose with a understanding that should have made us stronger, and wiser from those struggles. That can cause problems which could easily come from being weak in the process of those struggles. That if you not strong, those struggles will lead us to start making the wrong choices in life my brothers, and sisters no matter who you think you is. Plus on top of that if we do not go through struggles in life we want never learn how to be strong to make the right choices in life. Through whatever we go through, no matter if it is a struggle or not.

So now my brothers, and sisters we all should know that our struggles have meaning behind them, and they happen for a reason, with a purpose. That will allow you to become a better person from the right choices you make when those struggles come your way. Especially if we are in a relationship with the Lord. That will renew the strength in us all day by day. Where we want allow the weakness that is apart of the strength in us all, during our struggles to make the wrong choices. Even though my brothers, and sisters we still do sometimes, but like I said before, "it is for a purpose, and reason."

Now before I close this letter the Lord have informed me to tell my brothers, and sisters. That weakness from any struggles we go through in life must be manifested with strength before it can be perfected to make the right choices in life in anything we do. I submit and surrender my soul to you Lord.

Your beloved child
Jermaine Reaves

Dear Lord,

It brought tears to my eyes, that ran down my face, and all through my entire soul concerning my youngest daughter Brianna Jaliyah Reaves Lord. That every since she done grew up to have the mind to know, and understand Lord. She now beginning to realize that her father have not being there for the first four years of her life, and something is wrong, because she said to her mom Lord. "Why my dad not here with me on my birthday?" So smart as she is that kind of threw the moment off during her birthday party toward her family. That this little girl had full understanding that I haven't been there in years. That when she got a complete understanding that I will be gone some more years Lord. My little baby girl started making a wish on her birthday every year when she blow out her candles to bring her father home.

Plus not to mention when they took her to the shopping mall with the water spring in them. Especially the one's she notice where they had threw money in the water, and make a wish. Lord she started doing that as well, and the wish was the same, to bring her father home.

It is hurtful, and it really made me cry more and more to know that every time she made that wish for her father. It never happen for me at that time, but what I did realize was that my little baby girl had a whole lot of faith. That only can come from the Lord.

Lord I also found out through her mom that it really hurt her little heart. Which you already know Lord it going to hurt me just to know how much my little baby girl love her father. Who have not been in her life since she was three months old besides when she come visit me for a few hours. Which was a blessing for her, and me Lord, and that moment I truly realize it was you Lord standing in the gap for me. All these years for my little baby girl, and the rest of my kids, and love ones.

Thank you so much Lord, and I love you with all my heart, mind, and soul, but this moment is not about me. It is about my little angel, and beautiful little daughter Brianna Jaliyah Reaves.

That the world should know, and understand as I close this letter to you Lord. That my little baby girl started questioning her mother about what is the purpose of making a wish, and they never come true. Lord I cried for over a week about that.

Then after I talk to you through those trying times Lord. I said to myself Lord "this is a amazing, and a wise thing to know, and witness coming from a four year old child at that time" and the good thing about that Lord. I knew that you Lord had bless her little soul with that faith, and the mind to believe in her wish like I mentioned earlier.

Which is very good that the Holy Spirit is standing in the gap for me. That is already teaching her little spirit about faith, and she don't even know it, because every year that she think her little feelings getting hurt Lord. She never miss a year or gave up making those same wishes. Which is to please bring my father home.

She doesn't even know Lord her little faith, and belief is just getting stronger and stronger already, and it is such a blessing to know that she got faith she don't even know about. That also make her Lord believe in you, and me her father Jermaine Reaves.

It is just so amazing Lord to just be a witness, and apart of the power you have Lord working through her from those unanswered wishes. That soon will be answered in due time. Where I can hold my baby girl in my arms, and tell her that her wish have come true.

Proverb chapter 17 verses 6 says, "6 Children's children are the crown of the old men; and the glory of children are their fathers.

PS. Brothers and sisters these are the words of my precious little daughter Brianna Jaliyah Reaves. What is the purpose of making a wish if they never come true. I know you near us, and our kids Lord always.

Love always
your beloved child
Jermaine Reaves

Dear Lord,

Please bless me to be like the first king of the scriptures Melchizedek a leader with a heart tuned to God. Lord what about me being bless having the gifts of patient like Isaac had. Lord what about me being blessed with the gifts, and ability of leadership like Moses. Lord what about me being bless like King David a man after God's very own heart, and the greatest king of them all. Not to forget about being bless like Noah another great man of God with so much patient, consistency, and obedience for you Lord.

Lord how can I also be blessed with the ability like Joshua a strong Man of God with so much spiritual influence on people, and a strong leader for his people? What about being blessed with the strength, faith, will, and having the wealth like the man of God Job who lost everything, but gain everything back more abundantly believing in the Lord. What about if I was blessed like Samuel who lead the nation back to right living after all the evil what was going on in the world back then, and still going on now Lord. What about me being bless like Solomon the wisest man ever to live? Are also being blessed like Isaiah one of your great prophets, and a great deliverer of great messages concerning judgement, and hope.

Then there is Jeremiah the weeping prophet who I want to be bless like because of his act of faith despite all the things he went through in life. What about me being bless Lord like Daniel a man of prayers with the gift of prophecy. Then being bless like John the Baptist God appointed messenger who announce the arrival of Jesus Christ. Plus he was a great preacher about whomever theme was repentance. Then being bless like Paul who was transformed in his life by the Lord from being a persecution of Christian followers, to a great preacher who was led by the Lord to lead Christians to God despite his strong personality, and wrong living toward the Lord's children.

Then how can I be blessed like the greatest of them all you Lord. Our Lord and Savior Jesus Christ the most powerful, purest, and righteousness person ever to exist, and live in this world. Lord I know I can't be like you in every way, but I want to Lord. Lord I know it is impossible, and too powerful for anyone besides you Lord, but I do realize, and know one day everybody in this world going to know who you is Lord, and what you have done for us to still be here living in this world.

So we all can know, and understand some of our ancestors who I just name, and where we got our inheritance, abilities, and characteristics we carry in us from in so many ways. Which is up to us to use them the right way.

Now Lord I know you know that I want to be like you, and all the ancestors I name, and didn't name. That I can, and have, and will learn from in every way I possibly can, and know how. From you teaching me Lord everyday, and letting me know in the process that you Lord is with me. Where that I will keep striving to know that the Lord have also put in me my own gifts, abilities, and talents for the world. Through my purpose and the calling the Lord have put on my life for me in his own way. That is meant for me, and me only.

That will allow me to keep learning from every stage of righteousness from the Lord, our ancestors, the angel of heaven, my great brothers, and sisters that is rising up in this world to be great, and mighty men and women of God. Where we can unify, and do the work of the Lord in different ways, but the same purpose. Which is winning souls.

The Lord have told me writing to him to tell the world to apply everything you learn, and see to your life. Especially when you are learning, and seeing it on a spiritual level from God for your life. The Lord also said, "Jermaine Reaves you are, and will be a blessing to the people of the world with your own abilities, talents, and gifts. In away that I have gave you in your own way from what you been through says the Lord."

See since creation Jermaine Reaves everybody have affected the world in different ways, but in the end it will all be the same if it was affected the way that it was inherited in us all the right way from the wrong way.

So understand this, and take heed to it, and remember it for the rest of your life. That the world will learn from your old characteristics Jermaine Reaves as you being a ex drug dealer, living the life of going through so much violence, wrong choices, and bad decisions. Sleeping with so many different women. That could have caused me my life, but I was fortunately enough that I didn't catch a disease that is killing my brothers and sisters daily. Plus being shot are killed out there in the streets living the wrong way, and I can keep naming, but through the grace, love, and mercy of the Savior of this world. I was bless to make it through it all, and to change my life in some many ways. That have allowed me to acknowledge my purpose, and calling.

Even though I'm still a progress in work. The Lord still have let me know that I'm also a sanctified vessel coming from being incarcerated for years. That now carry a anointing from the Lord, and the teaching from learning from my great ancestors. That also include being healed, save, and delivered from the broken stages of my life. To now be a spiritual influence my own way that the world will witness, and never imagine coming from a person like me through you Lord. That was predestined to be release to the world.

Love always and forever
your beloved child
Jermaine Reaves

Dear Lord,

You know at time when you look out into the world Lord. I ask myself, "what do I see, and how far can I see Lord?" From all the things going on around me, and the world that I don't want to see.

So to my understanding, and the knowledge through you Lord. The answer was Lord that you have taught me to look beyond the condition of the world through my spiritual eyes.

That through you Lord I can now see further than what my natural eyes have seen, because the power of the spirit of the Savior of this world Jesus Christ have transformed my natural eyes sight to a spiritual eyesight. Which have allowed me to know, and see that what I see around me is temporary, and in due time will pass away.

So now that my spiritual eyesight have allowed me through the Lord to stay focus, and keep being prepared by the guidance of the spirit of the Lord. From a level beyond what I see in the natural, but see in the spirit. By these conditions from living up to the Godly principles of righteousness to the best of my well being, from my spiritual eyesight, and knowledge, understanding, and wisdom. Which is amazing, because the Lord have showed me through my spiritual eyes to look beyond the condition of this world through our Lord and savior Jesus Christ on a spiritual outlook. To know that the creator of this world is beyond what I see, and understand and what I cannot see, and will never understand. I know you near us always Lord.

Yours truly
your beloved child
Jermaine Reaves

Dear Lord,

You know that sometimes I have these moment in my life that challenge the knowledge in me. That have me asking you Lord to allow me to be able to define all stages of righteousness from being born as a born sinner from all my wrongs stages of living.

Even in the midst of the knowledge you put in me Lord to ask questions, because Lord I want to know, and I want the world to know too.

Why should we have to try to live on the path of righteousness everyday, and we was born naturally a sinner?

The Lord said, "the question was deep, but the answer is simple." Especially being in a relationship with me being taught by the knowledge I instilled in you from the relationship we have.

That you, and the world should know by now through the decision that was made in the beginning of creation from Adam, and Eve sin entered the world. That knock us all off a path that was perfect at the time. Which allowed us all to be born in this world from birth as born sinners, but on the day of the birth of the bright, and morning star. Which is our Lord and Savior Jesus Christ that direction change, and put us back on the path to not be perfect, but to know how to live in this world as a born sinner.

So through all the knowledge that the world have attained in so many ways about the Savior of this world. We all should know now that through the Lord and Savior death, and burial. That is the only reason that we are living in this world today to know how to live as born sinners striving through this journey that we call life.

Love always
Your beloved child
Jermaine Reaves

Dear Lord,

Striving on the path of righteousness is so hard, but it is truly worth it. So when we choose this path we should know that the path of righteousness is only so wide, but it is always enough room to move over for the next brother or sister who want to walk it with you. Plus we all going to need your help Lord, and each other help, because this path was not meant to be walked along, and definitely not for everybody.

Roman chapter 10 verse 20 Esaias said in bold words, "20 I was found by who did not seek me; I was made manifested to those who did not ask for me, but I am on the path of righteousness through salvation, and the grace of God for those who need me."

Psalms 23 versus 3 says, "3 He restoreth my soul: he leadeth me in the path of righteousness for his name sake."

Isaiah chapter 52 verse 15 also say, "15 But what had not been told them they shall see; and what they have not heard they shall consider, the path of righteousness through me, and the one who sent me."

If I can change my life, and get on the path of righteousness from the way I done lived Lord. I know they can too. Peace, love, and reverence to you always Lord.

Your beloved child
Jermaine Reaves

Dear Lord,

I love you, and I cry out to you Lord in prayers. I wrote this letter to you today to please ask you Lord to help us with our prayers, because majority of the prayers we pray is something we want or think we need. Instead of us being grateful with what you want for us, and have already bless us with in life. That really is meant for us to accept it, and pray for others.

Where we will realize that the thing we pray for dealing with what we think we deserve, and did not receive Lord. Most of the time we are to blind to see them, because it is not what we prayed for, because when you pray you need to be specific on what you pray for.

That is why I am writing this letter Lord to you for my brothers, and sisters Lord, because I want them to learn, and know that I'm a prime example of some of the thing I pray for. Due to me not knowing how to pray, because prayers not just based off what we need or want.

Then when we don't received the things we pray for by not being specific, and not to mention lining up to the will of God in the way God want for our life. It going to hurt you, because you think your blessings going to come from those prayers. So I just want my brothers, and sisters to know that about prayers.

So now since they know that. I can get to the direct message, and point of this letter to you Lord for my brothers, and sisters. Where they can understand everything we go through in life is for a reason. That will allow you to pray out of the will of God, and things that is not specific that God want you to have in your life.

So please understand that when we are praying for things which I don't know what everybody else pray for, but I do understand that prayer should have reverence, and repentance with thanks giving to the Lord every time we pray. Plus on that note we should also know that when we are praying our mind, and heart should be lineup to the will of God on what we should be praying about. Where we can see some results from our prayers, because brother and sisters in my case I been praying for the last 7 years for my freedom, and still haven't went home. It hurt, but I still keep praying, but in a specific, and different way. Especially when I'm asking God to take me home to my family from this incarceration.

See brothers, and sisters please understand that the God we serve knows what best for us all. So to summon this letter up, I realize, and you all should too brothers, and sisters that the Lord probably have not answered that prayer yet about me going home. I promise you all this my brothers, and sisters he have answered a whole lot of other prayers for me to be better when I do go home. Where I won't have to ever come back to prison again.

So please understand this, and take heed to the understanding of this letter to the Lord about prayers my brothers, and sister. That I'm not telling you to not pray for things you want or need. Just be specific, and line your prayers up to the will of God for your life, because the will God for your life going to happen anyway. Regardless of how you praying for things in your life.

Plus on top of that I'm just letting you know that God already done bless you with what you need, and going to have. So the more you pray the more you will realize we already bless with everything God want in our life. It's just up to us to use it, and accept them blessing the right way to get more, and more blessings in life from what we deserve, and want to have in life. By living the right way from our prayers, and being in a relationship with the Lord.

That will allow you to live by your prayers to get everything the Lord want you to have in life that you wouldn't never thought of, imagine, are understand. I love you always Lord, and know you are always near us.

Your beloved child
Jermaine Reaves

Dear Lord,

I was reading the daily bread in the month of May 2008, and I came across Philippians chapter 3 verse 7, and it said, "7 what things were gain to me, these I have counted loss for Christ", and one of the greatest thing came to my soul at that moment. That told me to ask you Lord. "What if I would have had a relationship with you Lord instead of all the women I done been with"? "What if I would have allowed my life to be rich with a soul fill with so much righteousness, instead of thinking I am rich in so many ways with all the money I got the wrong way, and wasted it Lord?" That now I can look back on my life, and just cry, and shake my head, and say to myself, "all that money gone now, the women gone, my so called friends gone, and on top of that you been gone away from everything you love for seven years.

Then I kept asking the Lord with tears pouring down my face. "What if I could have drove myself Lord deep into the chapters, and scriptures of the bible, instead of driving myself into the streets, and the so call drug game?" That didn't drive me to death which I was blessed not to end up that way, but it did drive me to being incarcerated for now seven years, and counting. Which when this incarceration is over, I'm still going to be label, and characterized as another black man that won't, and going to never be nothing. After I done paid my debts to society.

Then as I continued to cry through my tears I ask the Lord. "What if I could have went to church every week of my life, and pay my tithes, and bought the armor of righteousness, and kept them on

Lord. Instead of running to these malls buying clothes, shoes, jewelry, and some many other things that really didn't mean nothing to my life, but had me thinking I am so clean, I look good, and I'm all that."

Then Lord I ask you again, "what if I had spent half of my life devoting, and being inspired to strive in prayers, and fellowship?" Instead of spending all my time in the street wasting my life, and making so many wrong choices in life by not being myself, not being a good father to my kids, and just being all those bad things that I was, but really was not.

Now Lord through all my tears, and loneliness from being incarceration now for seven years, and counting. I done had a lot of time to think about so many things I been through in life I could have done the right way, but that question still come to me, "what if Lord?"

All I can do at that moment is just wipe my tears, shake my head, and tell myself Lord. That it wouldn't have last, because if it did. My life just would have been another wasted opportunity on something that I think I gain, but lost out on with the Lord, and everything else that was apart of my life.

So now that you can relate to this message by the way that the Lord have used me to write this letter.

Philippians chapter 3 verse 8 and 9 says, "8 Yet indeed, I also count all things loss for the excellence of the knowledge of Christ Jesus my Lord, for who I have suffered the loss of things, and count them as rubbish that I may gain Christ. 9 And be found in him having my own righteousness, within from the law, but that which is through faith in Christ, the righteousness which is from God by faith."

Thank you Lord, and I know we all will hear from you again. Everyday like we do, even when we don't know it, realize it, or care.

Love always
your beloved child
Jermaine Reaves

Dear Lord,

It amazed me that through the condition of me exercising my body all the time in a physical way. I done also learned that conditioning myself spiritually it so much better Lord, because conditioning yourself spiritually allow the physical aspect of your life to develop a whole lot better from just conditioning yourself physically. Why is that? because once you start conditioning your life spiritually your mind, heart, and soul going to develope better that is going to help the rest of your body. Especially when you using the right equipment.

Equipment that consists of a better understanding about life on a spiritual level. That is inspired by the love, and mercy of the Lamb of Judah. Which have instructed people soul with an exercise, that was a scarface, that cause death to a pure, and righteousness state of living from the son of God.

Who was born into this world by a spirit where the unrighteousness in us all can live the right way through him, that live as a human, and instructed the world to exercise their soul on a level of confession, and repentance.

Which will allow us to exercise our life by being obedient on a workout plan for our life that is made for everyone but lived out by some.

So we all got to understand that, when we start this workout plan don't never stop, because being instructed by the Lord you not only going to get the best results from the exercise program. Your life going to always get better day after day if you stay obedient.

Where you can live the right way, and go to the right place when this life is over.

Plus the Lord workout plan allow you to teach someone else by asking them to join you on this workout plan. That is instructed by the greatest instructor of this world the Lord, because the more you workout with the Lord exercise plan your body just not going to be right but your mind going to right. Your soul going to be right, and your heart is going to be right through the process from the Lord workout plan. That consists of a whole lot of strength. Which is a key part of the workout plan. That also consist of some powerful endurance. That will allow you to stay dedicated, committed, and determine. To get the best result that going to definitely last forever. I truly submit and surrender my soul to you always.

Love always
your beloved child
Jermaine Reaves

Dear Lord,

At this level of my life I'm beginning to come into being beyond my state of comprehension within myself. From the anointing on my life, and it is scary Lord, because sometimes I just do not understand it Lord.

So I'm going to allow my brothers and my sisters to be a witness. Where they can see what's in my soul, and they can let someone else have the opportunity alone with them to feel this powerful anointing that the Lord have place on my life. On a level through the divine presence from the Holy Spirit that is undeniable, and incredible.

That have summarize my life in so many ways as a man of God through the anointing on my life from the Lord. That through my soul, and the anointing the Lord have place on my life I got confident, and faith in the Lord. That after whoever reading this letter.

By the power of the Lord and Savior Jesus Christ a spirit of acceptance have moved inside of someone soul to change their life in so many ways. Dealing with fear, finances, loneliness, incarceration, drugs, abuse, neglect, love, division, discrimination, stress, work, and I can keep naming all other kind of situations, and circumstances that we all go through everyday living in this falling nation father God.

Lord you have showed me, and I truly believe through you Lord with faith, and the anointing on this letter from you Lord whoever read this letter. Somebody have overcame some of those stages they facing in life I just mention.

Which going to allow them to feel better, and change to take a step closer to you Lord. With a understanding, and a purpose by knowing that the Lord has sent this letter with this anointing on it from the Lord for someone else besides the one who God work through to write it. Where we all can overcome so many of these stages we face everyday in this fallen nation.

So please whoever you is, don't read this letter one time not even two time, but all the time. Why? because the more you read the words that come from the Lord, and being in the presence of this unique, and genuine anointing place on my life from the Lord, that you wouldn't imagine coming from a person like me. The more you will change to overcome some of the things you face in life everyday.

So please continue to be a witness with me from what just took place in your life from just reading this letter, and thank the Lord. For allowing a person you never thought or seen can have a anointing that can touch your life in away that you would have never thought.

That is why at this level in my life sometime I cannot even comprehend my anointing, but I know when the Holy Spirit appear. Trust me it is not of this world it's from the Lord, who is not of this world. Who made the world, me, and whoever reading this letter to understand. That this letter would have not even been written are read if it was not meant to be. I know you are near us always Lord.

Love always
your beloved child
Jermaine Reaves

Dear Lord,

I know through your words, and suffering you went through for us all to be here today Lord. No matter how unfair it was Lord.

It have help me, and I know it have help so many others to want to develop some strong characteristics about love. That can be a true blessing for so many other peoples through you Lord, because living for you Lord makes life productive, and fulfilling in ways that contagious, and affected toward other peoples dealing with love. Especially when we are feeling, and been treated the right way from the word love. Which have allow us all to know through the characteristics from the suffering the Lord went through for us all. That showed love beyond the meaning of the word love. Which is one of the most important thing we can not do, and that is stop showing love toward each other no matter what our differences is, because the Lord never stop loving us. Even when he was facing death on the cross.

Love always
your beloved child
Jermaine Reaves

Dear Lord,

Please help me stay grounded from the blessing that dwell in me from you Lord. That done grew to a level of acceptance that I never seen before in a way that done affected so many people's life Lord. By the power of your love, grace, and mercy. That done bless my life at this appointed time to overcome this incarceration, and every trials and tribulations of life I have encountered so far in life dealing with failures, and unrighteousness. Which have showed me that the more I strive, and grow staying in the presence of you Lord with the patient, and understanding from the spirit of the Lord. Through meditation, and praying. Studying, and writing, and searching everyday in my soul Lord. Have cause me to be unified within myself from my mind, heart, and soul on a completely different level that done affected everything around me. Plus to also know, and understand that my family have gotten better, because of you Lord making my life better, and they don't even know it yet.

Lord I also understand the world going to get better as well Lord through you using my life as a living testimony. Through the stages you bless me to overcome Lord. Where that I can stay grounded, and you Lord can continue to guide me to fulfill the purpose, and calling on my life on a level of life that have been bless to overcome so many stages of unrighteousness. Through the grace, love and mercy the Lord done showed me, and had on my life. Which done change me within to feel the same way in my soul toward the world and everything in it. From everything the Lord have brought me through to still be living in this fallen nation, and for this fallen nation today.

Thank you Lord for helping me stay grounded, and to have grown to continue to strive to complete my purpose, and calling in life through you Lord for the world.

Thank you again Lord so much for your love, grace, and mercy. Lord I love you, and please keep me grounded always, because I have truly submitted, and surrender my life to you Lord forever.

Love always
your beloved child
Jermaine Reaves

Dear Lord,

It is a true, and divine blessing to devote, and dedicate some time with you Lord. Where you Lord have gave me a peaceful spirit. That have allowed me to embrace some unbelievable things inside of me. That I feel that is so unexplainable on a level of respect that I can't help, but always needed, and truly wanted to have in my life for you Lord, and everything in the world. That now I got a full understanding about life that is so rememberable. Which have allowed me to realize in these moment Lord, my life is absolutely remarkable, and shareable.

Where that now in these moments Lord my soul is a witness to my life, and my life is a witness to the world that is filled with so much greatness within me from you Lord. That it is not even understandable, and to hold this moment of truth inside of me, and let it get away Lord without sharing it to the world is definitely not acceptable.

So at this moment Lord which is true. I ask you Lord, "to allow these moments within me to touch the world in ways that's incredible, and changeable."

The NIV bibles tell us in 1 John chapter 2 verses 24 and 25, and it says. "24 As for you, see that what you have heard from the beginning remains in you. If it does, you also will remain in the Son and in the Father. 25 And this is what he promised us-eternal life. I love you Lord, and I will always submit, and surrender my life to you now, and forever.

Love always
your beloved child
Jermaine Reaves

Dear Lord,

For years I use to hold grudges toward my so called friends, and love ones, and they know who I am talking about. The ones who have turned their back on me after all my life I tried to help everyone of them I considered my friends, and my family to the best of my abilities, and the only way I knew how.

Even though Lord the way I did help some of them was the wrong way especially from the way I use to live my life dealing drugs, because that is how I supported my life, my family life, and my friends life. By giving them drug money, and drugs to sell or whatever else I could give them to help them. From all kind of other negative ways, and things I did you can name ripping, and running the streets that definitely help them, but influence them in so many of the wrong ways.

See at the time Lord I thought I was making their life better, and all the while my life, and some parts of their life was getting worse, and worse. Then I realize Lord as I matured in the presence of you Lord, and striving on this journey of incarceration. At that time what I thought was helping me, those so call friends, and family members who turn their back on me. We really couldn't help ourselves, because we really wasn't ourselves, but some was, and some wasn't, because everybody know when you doing things for your family, and friend some of them appreciate it, and some of them just want to use you, and really don't care.

Lord you open my eyes up to a lot of things being incarcerated now going on seven years, and four months about the support of family, and friend. One thing was that they're not going to be there for you when you down, and out. Especially being incarcerated, but they know who I am talking about.

Lord I was hurt, and I carry that grudge toward them for years. Which I begin to understand in a relationship with you Lord that allowed me to know how to forgive, and let go, because life not going to stop for me or anybody else. Plus half of them probably can't even help themselves.

I do know who have been my only true, and honest friend that really have help me, and will always be there for me, and still here today for me after seven years, and four months of incarceration, and that is you Lord. Not to mention Lord some love one's, and they know who they are. I love you all, but so much have changed in them, and me. In some good ways, and some bad ways due to so much time spent being separated. Which will cause change in you no matter how much a person will say they been there for you or couldn't be there for you. It don't matter, because separation going to cause change whether they are there for you or not.

Lord you is my true friend that have made a difference in my life, and so many other peoples life. So I advise the world if you want a true friend in life. Be friend with the Lord who will never change on you, and will always be there, and that's what true family, and friends are for.

I can still say Lord, in so many ways I got four other friends besides the love, and friendship I got with you Lord. Which is my love, and friendship with Tasha, my mom, my kids, and my brother in some what way since he been home from being incarcerated for almost six years, and because of you Lord he made it. Then I got my friend Travis Hogan who I been friends with for over 20 years. Who I know, and God knows will always be my friend. Which I have been bless to talk to him on, and off on the phone for years, and through a letter he wrote me that was touching, and made some tears roll down my face. Then there is my long lost friend Eric Hubbard Lord. Who was amazing man, and apart of my life. That's was so important, because when I left him apart of his life left him and when he left me apart of my life left me. He told me on the phone one day when I call home from prison Lord, "Why I left him, and we cried together on the phone." I'm sorry my brother, and I love you. May your soul rest in peace, and in heaven, and I will see you again one day. I will always miss you my true friend who will live in my soul always.

Lord I can't forget about the brothers in Christ you allowed me to meet during this long journey of incarceration. Some true friends, and some true God fearing men that have inspired me to never give up, and help me when I had to struggle sometime when my love ones couldn't come through for me, and they know who I am talking about. Nothing, but love, and respect to them all.

So at this point in my life Lord I know, believe, and understand about true friends Lord, because true friends will last forever, and real friends will be with you through everything. Now since I know that Lord. I can share it to the world. Where we as people of the world will consider being in a relationship, and friendship with you Lord.

Now to those so call other friends, and love ones, and they know who I am talking about who turned their back on me. Please know that you all wouldn't real friends, and supposed to be my family anyway, and on top that you all did not really have no real love for me in the first place. I understand though, because the Lord done showed me, and taught me to not hold grudges, and to forgive you all, and to pray for you all. Where they can know in due time when I see them again we can still be associates instead of friends, and for my love ones to know that we are going to alway be family, but for them to understand that when they did turn their back on me. It allowed me to find my real friend, and real love one. Which is the best friendship I have ever had in my life, and that is with you Lord.

Love always and forever
your beloved child
Jermaine Reaves

Dear Lord,

I know through your teaching from the word of God, and the holy spirit Lord. Everything we do in life is not going to be easy, and everything we do in life is not going to be right. Lord I also know that we have all been born with the will in us to want to do right, no matter if we don't want to do right, because it is so hard trying to do right, when you want to do right without even trying to do right. Plus Lord I also know that everything going to be alright even if everything we want to do Is not right by trying to do it right.

Love always
your beloved child
Jermaine Reaves

Dear Lord,

I am at a stage in my life dealing with knowledge, and wisdom to really understand the condition of this world through you Lord. That I guarantee Lord that the condition we living in dealing with the way that life is with living. A lot of peoples don't understand Lord that these conditions been going on for so many generations, and years.

Conditions from generations, and years that this world if facing with healthcare. Conditions we facing with getting jobs, because at the time I was writing this book in 2008, the unemployment rate was at a all-time high. Plus the way that education is when after you done graduated from school, and college for so many years, and can barely find a job, but own the government money for going to school.

Then you got all these discriminating laws still going on that when you look around the world half of the brothers, and sister you grew up with or in your age range dying for no reason, going to jail for the rest of their life, and killing each other, because of no opportunities, and guidance.

Then on top of that, when you look around the world, everything we need in order to live, it's at an all-time high price wise. Things such as the clothes we wear, the food we eat, the gas we put in our car to get us to point A, and point B, our bills, and all type of things we need to live off of have been affected by the decision we make. The decision we can't help, and on top of that the decision these so call leaders in this country are making. Then the bad thing about that the money you work hard for they come back, and take most of that with these tax laws Lord.

See these just some of the conditions we face in this world for generations, and years, but it have now started to affect them now if you know what I mean. Don't get me wrong, because I am not racist. I am just telling the truth the way God want me to. Where the people of the world can take heed of what's going on around them, and been going on around them for years, and generations. Where they won't be so blind to the fact from not reading the word of God the bible. Where we all can get a the true understand about life living in a fallen nation. So my advice to you all every chance you get read the bible. Where you can see that these things been going on, and going to keep going on everyday for generations, and years.

Please understand this too that I am incarcerated, but the recession for the last eight years have affected the economy in ways we never witness or thought of, but it didn't affect the federal prison system. That did not go in no recession. So like I said before, "I guarantee that the peoples in this world Lord. Half of those peoples in this country do not care or realize that this have been like this in this world since creation and if you do not believe me you can read about it in the Book of Life. "Which is the bible. That will tell you about our ancestors who made a way for us, and went through the same things or even worser things back then. That lead up to right now dealing with these evil rulers that we continue to let sit on the throne around this fallen world, and if you don't believe me all you need to do is just open up your bible, and read, study, and ask the Lord for some understanding.

The bible is the tour guide for our life, and when you read some of them stories in the old testament, like I said "I guarantee you, you will see what I am talking about in this letter to the Lord for the world. "Plus while you are reading the bible ask the Lord to open up your spiritual eyes, mind, heart, body, and soul and see how some of those evil rulers back then affected this world for certain period of time over, and over again. So please open your spiritual eyes or your eyes period from being so blind. Where we all can make better choices with our decisions in theses modern time on who going to lead this country.

I pray, and hope that we will understand back then, and still today our great ancestors couldn't make their own choices back then, and look what happened. Which is still going on today, because if it wasn't this world would not be in the condition it's in now.

Plus understand this back then in the bible they called them kings, and judges, but now in modern times they are call Presidents. So just think about the Presidents we can remember, and what they did for the world when they was rulers in their countries, and understand what the Lord have allowed me to write to you all about the last eight years about the conditions we living in about the economy. That done affected us all, and our kids.

See the conditions I describe earlier was just some conditions we are facing peoples, and have been facing for generations, and years. Which II could have wrote about forever, but why, and what going to change if we don't make the right choices when we deciding who going to lead this country. Really it matter, but not for me, because for one I can't decide due to me being a felony. So my rights been take, but I know, and understand who going to lead me, and that is the Lord. I also hope after you read this letter you will let the Lord lead you as well, and start living your life by the bible. Which is the true, and living word of God.

So please decide who going to lead you in this country, and not your life, because no matter who you is or how old you is all our decisions make a difference.

That is why this country have been bless with a good king to lead the peoples of this country. Who some of peoples of this world thought in their mind, something like this will never happen, but like I been taught to learn from the spirit of the Lord you cannot stop what was meant to be from the Lord. See the Lord know that the peoples in this country have suffered enough for the last eight years. Not to mention generations, and years. So please do not take your eyes of the Lord peoples, because this new king now sit on the throne for America to lead us out of somethings that I know will be better if they let him for a certain period, and time,

Thank you Lord, and I hope they all know this, and take heed to it. That you is the Lord and Savior of this world Jesus Christ who sit on the throne of creation not for a certain period, and time but always and forever.

In closing, now after eight years the Lord have bless us with a good king to lead us, but we got to be in unity, and play our part to make this country a better place by helping our leader make better decision so the condition in this country, and the World can get better, and will get better for us, our kids, and the generation to come.

Love always and forever
your beloved child
Jermaine Reaves

Dear Lord,

Dealing with this incarceration Lord I have had time for seven years, and four months to peep down in my soul through you Lord. That have allowed me to see some interesting things. That I truly didn't know about myself, and definitely did not understand about myself as well. It starts with dealing with this incarceration Lord, which have now been seven years, and four months.

Lord what I witnessed, and seen in my soul was still a lot of hurts, and pains that I thought I got over. From what I been through in my life that over the course of this journey of incarceration Lord. Your love, mercy, and grace have helped me heal in a lot of ways from those hurts, and pains dealing with my past, but still come up sometimes that try to make me lose focus. Why Lord? I do not know, but I do know through you Lord, you have allowed me to stay focused, and change. Where I can move on in life from those hurts, and pains when this incarceration is over.

So that I can continue to live in a committed relationship with you Lord. That have establish me to be a better man from being save, renewed, stronger, and always encouraged by the words of God. Plus being dedicated, and determined to stay that way when this incarceration is over.

Which through these long, and trying times of this incarceration for now seven years, and four months it allowed me to get closer, and closer to the Lord, and as I got closer, and closer to the Lord. I got deeper, and deeper. Which allowed everything I was dealing with inside of me to be set free without any more regrets, and worries, and in the process.

The Lord allowed me to also realize in my soul, and for me to see all my losses, and what caused them. So through the process the Lord taught me to understand that those losses was a gain to my life dealing with the way I use to live. That if I would have kept living that way from all those ungodly stages of life I would have lost out on life, and wouldn't have never gain back my life with myself, my kids, my wife to be, my family, and my relationship with you Lord.

That is why I am so grateful Lord to be able to let all my brothers, and sisters know that when you got a special relationship with the Lord. You can go deep within yourself, and realize some amazing life changing things. That have let me know, and understand that what happen to me was for a reason, because if it wasn't for this incarceration I would have lost out on everything.

Which would have allowed me to never know through the Lord I was anointed to write to the Lord for the world. That is so interesting, so attracted, so unique, so important, so real, so true, so great, and so understanding, because the Lord let me know through this incarceration he was not looking for no more excuses from me. From my losses, my hurts, my pains, and everything I been through in life.

So what I did lead by the holy spirit I started writing to you Lord. Which I write to you for the world, but also for myself, because the things I been through in life. The things I seen on this Christian journey, and this journey of incarceration this is what happen, because things we go through in life is for a reason.

Please read Isaiah 55 verse 5 and it says, "5 Surely you shall call a nation you do not know, and nations who do not know you shall run to you because of the Lord your God, and the Holy one of Israel; for he has glorified you."

Isaiah 60 verse 15 says, "15 Whereas you have been forsaken and hated, so that no one went through you, I will make you an eternal excellence, a joy of many generation." Thank you Lord Jesus I love you always.

Your beloved child
Jermaine Reaves

Dear Lord,

Thank you for the strength to continue to strive in this christian journey. A journey in life that everyday while you are living in this world you going to have to fight these battles. Even though the war been won through our Lord and Savior Jesus Christ the battles continues on.

Then there is time even when we are fighting these battles we face in life dealing with ways we live now from the way we have changed. We still feel like we are losing these battles sometimes Lord. Then there is time we done fought that battle hard in life dealing with change, and nothing seem like it have change Lord. Which will allow you to want to give up, and get off the battlefield. After all that fighting Lord, but at that moment.

That is when you always come in Lord, and remind me that you already won the war, and for me to just keep fighting in the battle. You also Lord remind me to always remember what you taught me. What you brought me through, and for me to always know that you is with me always. Plus to keep the armor on, because you going to need it everyday fighting in this spiritual warfare.

So we should never think we at a level in life where everything going good in our life, and we got to stop fighting on the battlefield, because before you know it or realize it, those good things you got going on in your life is gone. Whatever it is, how much it is, and who it is, because you stop fighting on the battlefield. that is why it is so important we keep fighting, and not be content, because time you stop fighting in the battle for the right reasons for the Lord. You're not only going to lose the battle for yourself, but you also going to lose the battle for your kids, your family, love ones, everything you fought hard for, and all the brothers, and sister you could have help if you would have kept fighting.

So please understand that the war been won but the battles continues like I said before, but know when them battles come, and you still fighting them for the Lord, and the world. You will get rewarded on how you fought, and what you was fighting about. So take my advice fight for what is right for the Lord, and trust, and believe that what you was fighting the battle have already been won.

Love always
your beloved child
Jermaine Reaves

Dear Lord,

I love you, and I am so grateful that you Lord have blessed me with another opportunity to be used through you Lord. To deliver a message in this letter from my soul again lead by the Holy Spirit with the anointing you have put on my life to let the people of this world know that. We value life more fully when we been blessed to overcome the stages of life from whatever it may be dealing with captivity, and I am not talking about the captivity from being incarcerated.

I am talking about the captivity that take place in our mind, our heart, our body, and our soul, and the messed up thing about that Lord somebody go through it everyday, and they be the people you will never think or imagine. Due to the fact from who they is or what they got, but deep down inside of them most of them from within their inner self is in captivity, and need to free theyself through being in a relationship with the Lord.

See in the word of God the word say, "who the son set free they is free indeed."

Then on top of that if we do not unlock whatever captivity going on inside us mighty Lord we going to miss the purpose in our life because, what lay in the deepness part of our soul is a precious jewel. That is so valuable to each other life, and the world, and if we do not use it the right way Lord it is a cost to us, each other, and the world.

So brothers, and sisters unlock yourself, because you might be laughing on the outside, but crying on the inside. Which will cost you to never use the jewel inside you, and reach your destiny.

Love always and forever
your beloved child
Jermaine Reaves

Dear Lord,

I know that all of my wrong ways of life I done lived, and my brothers and sisters I know done lived, are should I say, "seen live the wrong way Lord." I have learned that it was not worthy it, and I am so grateful to still be here to understand that you can never take nothing in your life for granted.

So now that I have had another chance in life to get it right through this long journey of incarceration for years. Lord you have truly taught me to know through growing older, and maturing in this journey in life being in a relationship with you Lord. Some of them wrongs ways I was living that cause me to get incarcerated Lord. You said, "it save my life, and you Lord have help me overcome so many wrong stages I was living in the wrong way. From this incarceration that have gave me the opportunity to still be here living. Me, and some of my brothers, and sisters who have encountered so many wrong ways of living as well.

The sad thing about that Lord is that, the one's they said wouldn't going to be here is still here, and the one's you thought should be here is gone. Which is the reason we can never take nothing in our life for granted, "like I said before."

So Lord you have let me know if it was not for my wrong ways that I have lived I wouldn't even be here at this point in my life. Incarcerated or not to be writing no letters to you Lord about my life.

Plus I wouldn't even have had the opportunity to be striving in a relationship with you Lord. Which have gave me a reason to know my purpose in life, and on top of that. I wouldn't have knew nothing about praying, writing, self control, peace, patient, and I can keep naming, but what is the most important thing the world should know about Lord I probably won't be living.

Thank you Lord for life, and helping me continue to prepare myself through this incarceration, and these trying times that we all going to face everyday. Thank you also Lord for the anointing that you have place on my life from being incarcerated. Thank you Lord for teaching me about my talents, and gifts, that is been read right now through what I done lived through from so many wrong ways of my life. Thank you Lord for saving me from myself. Thank you Lord.

Love always
your beloved child
Jermaine Reaves

Dear Lord,

You told me to always write to you about what's on my mind, and in my heart, and soul. So Lord this question, and this letter I am writing to you Lord. When the people of this world read it they might think I am crazy.

Lord you know that I am a true man of God, and a God fearing man, and share not no Satan fearing man. So Lord is it truly possible for a person like me to figure out the mind of Satan? and why I ask that question Lord it is for so many reason.

Reason Satan have cause in our life always dealing with brokenness, and hardship. Which we all have been through in life letting Satan control our heart, mind, and soul by living our life on the stage of unrighteousness. Why I ask that question Lord is, because I know you done bless me, and many others to stand up for the people of this world, and just the world in general for so many reason.

For one Lord, it is time for the world to know, and understand that I am tired of Satan. I want to figure out a way through you Lord to eliminate his chances from this point on in my life, and in the world. Now, and forever. Where he can stop destroying us, our family, and the people of this world by using so many ways of life that we know, see, and understand, but won't do nothing about it.

Lord these ways consists of choices we make. People we deal with. Situations, and circumstances we go through, and so many other different ways of life Satan put in front of us. That he disguise to make look good, and worth our while on all levels of life Lord, and these tactics from Satan, because we are not being mindful. These ways are destroying us, separating us, abusing us, neglecting us, rejecting us, and I can keep naming so many other ways Satan have affected our life living unrighteousness.

So since I'm at a whole different level in my life where I been truly bless to know the Lord personally. The Lord have absolutely bless me with so much intelligence, knowledge, wisdom, and understanding about Satan, and about life.

Even though Satan have, and still is destroying the life of so many people in this world everyday, and it hurt me so bad, because I know what I want to do about it, but I know in so many ways I can't do nothing about it, and that is to kill him. Which is impossible, because we all know he still powerful, still conceiving, convincing, conniving and always hurting, and killing our brothers, and sisters opportunities in life to change, and want to be better everyday, and all day.

Which now I want the world to know this too it is not what I can do it is what the Lord can do, and have already done. See the Lord done taught many of us about Satan, and I feel that everybody in this world have that understanding, but the sad thing about that we do not use it, and that is why Satan going to continue to seek, kill, and destroy.

So until we get bold, and want to figure out the mind of Satan learning from the Lord like we was created to be toward Satan ways, and tactics. All Satan going to do is continue to go to, and fro destroying the things we love. That is why it is time for us to use the knowledge the Lord bless us to have where we can save ourselves, and others in this world.

Whoever is reading this letter I am asking you to please start right now spending some devotional time getting to know the Lord better, and ask him that same question. Is it possible for me Lord to figure out the mind of Satan? and when the Lord give you the answer. It will be up to you to put your mind to do what the Lord tell you to do, and I guarantee this through the trust, and faith I have in the Lord. That all our answer will line up the same, and that answer from the Lord will be I will control your mind, and Satan mind if you obey me, and I will give you the mind to figure out his mind, because he got to obey me.

Love always
your beloved child
Jermaine Reaves

Dear Lord,

I ask you to give my thoughts so much understanding that is beyond a level of knowledge, and wisdom that is better than my own thinking through you Lord using me lead by the spirit of intelligence from the Holy Spirit for this world from my mind.

Lord give me a heart beyond the feeling of true love from the Holy Spirit that this world have never seen or felt since you Lord walk the face of this earth so many years ago. Where that we can accept that love without jealousy, and envy that will change lives through you Lord using me in this world from my heart.

Lord give me a soul from the Holy Spirit beyond the emotional let down through my tears from what I been through that is undeniable, and impossible for the people of this world no matter who they is, what they think, and how they feel about me. It won't stop this world from getting better from my soul.

Lord now that you have given me these things in my mind, my heart, and my soul let it now come to past. Where in due time I can see what I wrote through you Lord for the world years from now. Which will allow me, and others to know that what you reveal to me from this journey of incarceration, and staying in the presence of the Holy Spirit in the process have come true, and the prophecy you bless me to have within myself have been full fill.

Where the world will see it, accept it, respect it, and believe it. To really know that the Lord put all this inside of me, and the outcome was truly what the Lord said it was going to be," miraculous". Which going to allow me to be stronger, and more encourage to continue the mission. From the purpose, and calling the Lord have blessed me with for the world. Truth, and honesty always Lord.

Love always
your beloved child
Jermaine Reaves

Dear Lord,

I have open my spiritual eyes in every way through you Lord. That have allowed me to now understand the things I can see beyond the condition of this world, and all my iniquities, and transgressions. That have been a lesson, and a blessing that can be explain in many ways, and also understood by all, because like Ephesians chapter 3 verse 19 says, "19 To know the love of Christ which passes knowledge-that you may be filled with all fullness of God.

Lord that verse should definitely give us insight from what we see, and what we go through. Plus on top of that we should now have definition, and understanding about life, that we all strive for, and look for from you Lord. That now we can understand, and comprehend a lot better to know, and look beyond what we see, and look forward to what we don't see. Plus what we see we all should know that everything around us is temporary accept God, and his words, and what we do not see we should know, and if we do not know that everything we do not see is eternal like God, and his words.

Hebrew chapter 11 verse 1-3 says, "1 Now faith is the substance of things hoped for, and the evidence of things not seen. 2 For by it the elders obtained a good testimony. 3 By faith we understand that the world was framed by the word of God, so that the things which are seen were not made of things which are visible.

P.S. Brothers, and sisters this my letter to the Lord for you all from my spiritual eyes. That in due time the things I see within my soul from the Lord I have confidence, and faith that the people of the world who is living for the Lord in a true, and righteousness way will witness what many others want to see.

Love always and forever
one of your beloved children
Jermaine Reaves

Dear Lord,

   This book is a revival, and a life changing journey for me that I wrote these letters to you Lord for the world through this journey of being incarcerated for almost eight in a half years. On all the levels of life I been through living the wrong way for all the wrong reason. To now being saved, and blessed through the process. That have allowed me to be in a relationship with the Lord, and discover my calling, and purpose in life.

   Which have put a special feeling in me, and send chills down my body. That is is covered with a anointing, and educated by the Holy Spirit that I know, and believe in God, and in my heart this book from my life is truly a blessing that is needed for the world.

   Before I end this book with a bonus letter to Lord. I just wanted to share to world the amazing power from the Lord that have affected my four year old daughter. Who wrote letters to her father the best way she can, and the amazing thing about that the words was clear to me, because of the way they was express. I know that the Lord lead her, and some might not believe, but these letters are from a four year old kid my daughter Brianna Jaliyah Reaves.

   Dear Dad,

      I put all my money that my mom and grandmother and other people give me and put them in an envelope to send to you dad and then I will ask my mom how much it is to get you out where you can come home and help me.

Love always
Brianna Reaves

Dear Dad,

I make wishes on my birthday and every time I go to the mall I make wishes also and throw my money in the wishing well and wish that you will come home dad and since my wishes have not came true I ask my mom one day dad what the purpose in making a wish and it never come true.

Love always
Brianna Reaves

Dear Dad,

My mom told me that my uncle Chris is coming home and I told her that is good but I don't want to hear about no one coming home but my dad.

Love always
Brianna Reaves

Dear Dad,

Sometimes I just wake up screaming and crying about you dad. Then my mom will ask what is wrong and all I can say is I want my daddy.

Love always
Brianna Reaves

BONUS LETTER

Dear Lord,

It is so amazing to be bless with a anointing that is so true, so honest, and so real dealing with so many hurts, and pains. So much loneliness, and losses. Trails and tribulation, worries and I can keep naming Lord, but through them all Lord you have bless me to realize that there is something great in me. That is unbelievable that a person like me can be apart of you Lord to be so anointed with a spirit that is unsearchable, undeniable, unique, and so understandable. That every time you turn the page of this book you can feel the spirit of the Lord that dwell in my soul, and the most amazing thing about that it connects with the hearts, minds, and souls of the people of this world that was blessed to read THE WINDOWS OF INSPIRATION THROUGH THE REVELATION OF INCARCERATION FROM JERMAINE REAVES AND THE LORD. So to the world I give my love, my honor, and the glory to you Lord. Thank you Lord, and thank you all, and please Lord continue to bless my soul, and keep me humble. Where that I can always strive in a relationship with you Lord with this anointing that you have embrace me with to continue to spread what you have done for me to the world. That going to cause so many changes in others life. So much love, and unity in the the world forever, and always. I love you Lord.

P.S. Please brothers, and sisters open up your Bible before you close this book and read LUKE chapter 4 verses 14-22 and it summarizes some of the purpose, and calling of this book, and my life through the Lord.

Yours truly
your beloved child
Jermaine Reaves

Printed in the United States
By Bookmasters